THIS IS WHAT I HEARD

IGNITE YOUR DIVINE SPARK

ASCENSION COMMUNITY

Copyright © 2022 Ascension Community

All rights reserved. No portion of this book may be reproduced in any form without permission from the publisher, except as permitted by U.S. copyright law.

ISBN: 979-8-9862411-1-1

CONTENTS

FOREWORD | *CALVIN STREETE*	1
FOREWORD | *MARK P. GREGORY*	2
ACKNOWLEDGMENTS	3
THE ASCENSION COMMUNITY	7
CHOSEN | *LINDA "LINLIN" HOOKS*	11
A MOMENT OF CLARITY | *MELISSA CLAUDIO*	24
THE "IN" GAME | *TANGENIQUE KING*	36
JOURNEYING BACK TO THE SELF | *NINA CURTIS*	46
SEEING THE WOOD FOR THE TREES | *RACHAEL EBANKS-GOLD*	58
I EXIST AS WE, WE EXIST AS I | *KIMBERLY GARDNER, PH.D.*	72
TAPESTRY | *EQUINE "EQ" SHEFFIELD*	85
THE INNER WORK | *DR. NAZLI FOULADI*	94
THE JOURNEY WITHIN | *ROMANA BEAUCHAMPS*	105
TWO SIDES OF THE SAME | *LINDSEY D. AHERN*	116
REFERENCES	128

FOREWORD
by Calvin Streete

Welcome!

I know you feel lost, but we actually found you. You may be experiencing a void, displacement or are unsure of yourself. You want to go back to what's familiar. The uneasy look on your face is the mourning of your former self but also the freedom from a bonded existence. You are now in the company of the initiated--those who share your journey-- and we will light the way to help lift a burden that is heavy on the soul. There is one of us born into every family, and we are chosen to help the acceleration of humanity, and you are the one.

As a collective, we are here to imprint our energy and to ignite your divine spark. We all share that spark and soon you will too. *Who are you? Where are you? Why are you here?* If these questions have echoed in your mind and heart since you arrived, I believe we are here to assist. We have found you but now *you* must find *you*. We will walk that journey with you as we share our light and become transparent. However, we must ultimately walk through the door ourselves.

Open your mind to these expressions and experiences. These star seeds are an inspiration in this spiritual war. Generators, operators, and destroyers of old paradigms, they are now recreating themselves into their own image. I welcome you to a higher dimension of awareness--a world unknown to many but chosen by those who desire change. You will feel at home here and will surely find your true family. Exhale as we embark on a journey to discover our inner divine selves.

FOREWORD
by Mark P. Gregory

In the journey of life, billions of thoughts pass through our minds. These thoughts, or what we hear, ultimately dictate our actions. I believe it is important that we take time to deconstruct these thoughts and find their origin.

As humans, we are multi-dimensional. We have a past, live in the present, yet strive for the future. Many people cannot enjoy the fullness that life has to offer because they are haunted by the past. Their decision-making is marred by the subtle whispers of hurt, pain and disappointment. Past traumas spill into our present lives to the point that we get stuck in this cyclical pattern of negative self-talk.

This is What I Heard illuminates the presence of divine messages people hear when they do introspective work and allow a greater power to guide them. Doing so may not erase the past, but can ensure a better future.

As you move forward, retrain your mind to understand that stillness is okay. It is important that, in this stillness, you not just hear but also trace the root to some of those pesky thoughts. In this book, you'll find a compilation of stories from individuals whose journeys led them to peel back layers of past experiences and pains. Each of them endured a process to uninstall old, noisy programs.

Enjoy reading about the discoveries they made along the way. They'll tell you all about how "this is what I heard" became a mantra to help them ignite their divine spark.

ACKNOWLEDGEMENTS

If we're lucky, we get to spend time co-creating with people who continuously inspire us. I am so lucky to have connected with a bunch of those people.

To the Ascension Community Members:

Without the experiences and support from members of the Ascension Community, this book would not exist. Through the many shares, gifts, and talents you have given and continue to give, you inspire others to continue their path of ascension.

To the Ascension Community Contributing Authors:

Thank you for being transparent and willing to express "This is what I heard" moments with us in text. Healing happens through your shared experiences. Thank you for being an inspiration to so many. We did it!

To the Ascension Community Club Admins, Leaders, Moderators (and their families):

All the forests in the world could not produce enough pencils to write how much appreciation I have for the hours of dedication, time, energy, and breath you have given to the community. Thank you for hosting, moderating, and managing dialogue in the many chat rooms we've created. I am grateful for your families who allow us to borrow some of their time with you. Without your support and continuous love, the Ascension Community would not be as magical as it is today.

SPECIAL ACKNOWLEDGEMENTS

Amir Lester-El – I'd take up all the air in the universe to be able to fully express my gratitude for your love, support and for choosing me to be your Earth mom. Thank you for introducing the community to the book, *Frequency: The Power of Personal Vibration*, by Penney Peirce. Lives were changed for the better because of your love and generosity.

Tangenique King and Melissa Claudio – To the "council" who know without words how much appreciation I hold for the many hours of deliberation, tears, chuckles, and creative moments you have given to the community and this book project. It's easy to see the results of hard work when it appears on the surface, but it's a different view from the trenches. Thank you for being in the trenches and holding the vision in sight.

Christine Racheal Wilson of Airris Books – I offer my profound gratitude for your superb and straightforward editing approach, probing questions and creative flare which made this book better than first imagined.

Calvin Streete – Thank you for the incredible value you add to the Ascension Community rooms and for writing such an inspiring foreword.

Alpha Exploration Co. (dba "Clubhouse") – I wish to express my appreciation to the founders of "Clubhouse" for creating a wonderful platform that allows people to find their tribes from all over the world.

Alex Johnson Productions – I would like to extend my profound appreciation for the comprehendible translation you offer of the sacred text, *The Diamond Sutra*.

Mark P. Gregory (Comic Mark Greg) – Thank you for your amazing support and friendship. You heal the world through laughter and love. Thank you for pouring some of that love into a beautiful foreword for this book.

Kerwin Claiborne – I appreciate the love and support by sharing this book with your millions of followers on social media. You bring joy and laughter to so many. Thanks for helping to raise the vibrations in the world through humor, and for allowing many to become aware of this beautiful book.

Equine Sheffield – Thank you for your amazing support, advice, and audio book donation to the community.

Special Thank You's

I would like to pay tribute to the many people who have given freely of their time, hearts, and energy to help this book come to fruition.

Tangenique King – Cover Art Concept, Content Reviewer
Christine Racheal Wilson (Airris Books) – Cover Design, Editor
Linda Hooks & Melissa Claudio – Project Managers
Mark P. Gregory and Calvin Streete – Forewords

AUTHORS

Equine Sheffield
Kimberly Gardner, Ph.D.
Linda Hooks
Lindsey Ahern
Melissa Claudio
Dr. Nazli Fouladi
Nina Curtis
Rachael Ebanks-Gold
Romana Beauchamps
Tangenique King

The Vision

Linda "LinLin" Hooks created the Ascension Community after having a vision of a bartering community where the community members would trade their natural gifts and talents. LinLin saw that everything we use in the world is powered by human beings, from the machines made to manufacture products and government and financial systems to the buildings, retail stores, and banks that allow for trade and commerce. Everything requires the energy of human beings, and she saw this as an unlimited supply of energetic currency. The "middleman" wasn't involved in her vision as people traded their natural abilities with other human beings. Since the "middleman" (banks, retail stores, etc.) was not present, people didn't require money to acquire things. Instead, the new currency was the love and joy of one another. Bartering could happen in a neighborhood or amongst families on a small scale, and people worldwide could share their gifts and talents virtually or in-person on a larger scale.

The Beginning

The critical component of the barter exchange would be that each person enjoys the service they offer. In turn, this high-vibration activity would raise the frequency in the world as people would be happy doing what they love and serving others in the process. LinLin decided to start discussions around this in 2018 with people in her area.

The COVID-19 pandemic moved people to adhere to

"lockdowns" where they were not allowed to gather in person or in large groups. As the government advised that non-essential workers remain at home, many began to work from home. While this may seem like a disruption to LinLin's vision, it led her to discover an audio-based social media app called Clubhouse, which allowed her to facilitate these discussions with people worldwide.

As talks began, LinLin quickly realized the benefit of allowing the community to form organically and based on each member's conscious awareness. While the bartering component is still being revealed, community members continue to naturally grow together as they all awaken to the divinity within them. This is what we call the ascension journey, and we realize more of our divine nature within and find connections between everything and everyone around us.

The Growth

The members of the Ascension Community are a group of dynamic human beings from all over the world. The community first opened its doors on Clubhouse in the summer of 2021 and, by December of the same year, had attracted over 1,500 members worldwide. Rooms are hosted every week on any topic that encourages people on their journey. Rooms have included book readings and discussions, movie and music break-downs, and host special guest speakers, authors, musical artists, nutritionists, and leaders from around the world.

The Culture

The Ascension Community takes pride in having a beautiful space where people can be themselves, be weird, vulnerable, authentic, and not judged. First time-visitors who enter the rooms of the Ascension Community Club echo this sentiment. LinLin built a Clubhouse Moderator Training Program, which allows leaders and administrators to help others develop their skills in moderating rooms while in the community. This aids in maintaining the consistency of love and respect participants feel regardless of which room they attend. The community practices a monthly act of generosity and peace called "Gen Zen" to raise the vibration in the world by completing heartfelt acts of charity and peace. You'll often find members sporting the Ascension Community logo as a part of their profile avatar to express unity and oneness as they participate in rooms together.

The Next

The Ascension Community is excited to realize a full-functioning bartering community in the future. In addition, there are plans to publish more books, launch a radio show, offer retreats, community outreach projects, and more!

We invite you to get to know us and grow with us. Visit us at **https://www.ascensioncommunity.org**. There is great love, joy, and healing here for you.

THIS IS WHAT I HEARD

CHOSEN

LINDA "LINLIN" HOOKS

Born in Newark, New Jersey to a very talented family, Linda Hooks (affectionately known as LinLin), has traveled all over the world doing what she loves. Whether performing as a singer in Italy, Austria or Switzerland, having a conversation about intuition in the "hot seat" at an Abraham Hicks workshop, or presenting her perspective on an Oprah Winfrey Network television special, Linda has always been extremely good at one thing--being herself.

Today, she is an impactful Transformational Speaker and Coach who takes pride in helping others break through the illusions and stories they've told themselves about lack. Her work helps guide people to freedom by pointing them to the divine power within. Wherever she goes, she becomes the chosen one that people seek for advice. The reason? She enjoys people's excitement when they remember who they are as unbound beings.

LinLin is the visionary and creator of the Ascension Community, which is a place where people are able to be themselves, tell their stories and drop the weight they've carried around for years.

She is the proud mother of two extremely talented children who inspired her life's work and this book.

INSPIRATION

I choose myself fully and I accept my power.
-- Linda "LinLin" Hooks

Life, to some, is all about images and perceptions. Images control perceptions. In 2018, much of the world lived on the internet and social media, which are buried in images, edited videos, and skewed perceptions. When I spoke with a friend about a vision I had of a bartering community, I had no idea that a few years later it would lead me to another social media application (app). Needless to say, I was skeptical at first but my vision was strong.

In this vision, I saw people utilizing their natural gifts and talents to trade the things they absolutely love to do. This community operated in a beautiful energy of love and service--trading skills in cooking, gardening, mechanics, artistry, babysitting, carpentry, and more. After sitting on this vision for a couple of years without doing anything more than creating a Facebook page, I came across an app in 2021 called Clubhouse.

Clubhouse is an audio-based app that feels like a virtual conference room. I figured it would be a great place to begin conversations about the bartering community. I opened the Ascension Community Club on Clubhouse and began the journey. I had no idea how the community would evolve or that it would begin to reveal itself as a greater awareness of our souls' nature.

During this time, I was already quite aware of my spiritual journey. I've always been an intuitive person, so when the bartering community came to mind, I sensed that it would involve my own spiritual growth, as well as other people who were also on a path of ascension toward greater consciousness and love.

THIS IS WHAT I HEARD

Throughout my life, I've received visions, random ideas or knowings about things even before it happens. My mother told me that I was like my grandmother who also had an intuitive and discerning spirit and could sense things with ease.

Sometimes, the "knowings" would steer me out of harm's way. Other times, it served as a guide through uncharted territory of my life's path. The idea for the community happens to be one of those times when I knew I was getting a glimpse of something that would come in the near future. When the vision came to me of a large community of happy people who live abundantly by sharing and trading the things they love to do, I knew intuitively that it was very special and it would be part of a major, emerging paradigm shift in the world. This shift would force its' members to trade the controls they had learned and become accustomed to over the years for a very different world we can all come to know and enjoy. I, too, would not be immune to this shake-up. I could tell that this community would push me to be on purpose, and with greater purpose. So far, the Ascension Community has helped me realize that when we choose to surrender to our soul's purpose, it grows us.

> "I had no idea how the community would evolve or that it would begin to reveal itself as a greater awareness of our souls' nature."

In a vibrational world, you can't have what you're not willing to become. A community of this magnitude would require its members to dissolve old ways of being to align with a higher frequency of harmony, prosperity, and wholeness.

The process of transformation is inevitable, and everyone will experience it. The question is: on what frequency will we choose to experience it?

Today, technology controls how humans see the world. Television screens all over the world are flooded with visuals and news of death, crime, war, corruption, poverty, disease and lack. Movies appear to move us toward a world where machines replace the human touch. Thankfully, I am beyond the indoctrination of mainstream media and religiosity. I've moved on to enjoying an ungoverned and quite candid relationship with who I call God, Source, Soul, and All. My world is very different, and it doesn't match the images and reports that appear on television or the internet. In my vision, I see love. I see abundance everywhere. I see people doing work without it feeling like work. I see people caring more about what their soul wants and less about what others think. I see people being generous and peaceful with one another.

All it takes, as my son says, is to simply "choose love". Choosing love is an easy choice, as my daughter says, when we simply "be love". These are very insightful views from two young adults whose lifetime has been dominated by the old paradigm of greed, capitalism, and vanity. I heard somewhere that the love of God operating in the human heart is unconditional. Well, this way of thinking is certainly not society's norm. Life is now forcing us to dissolve the things of the old and evolve into a new way. Yes, it's a new day.

What does it mean to break away from the old paradigm and choose the path of ascension?

For me, it means making a choice to be chosen. Just as we chose to be here on Earth at this incredible time in human history, we are choosing every day to either evolve in consciousness or hold on to the dense world that is presented to us. While in the Ascension Community, I came to understand that I was making the choice to ascend. As I became more familiar with Clubhouse, I realized that the only images on the app are the profile pictures or avatars of the app's users.

One morning, I joined a chatroom and listened to a group of people discuss a book that was considered the oldest, dated, printed text in the world. The book entitled, *The Diamond Sutra*, is also known as the Diamond that cuts through all illusions. In the room, I kept hearing about Buddha, and I thought, "Oh dear, here we go with another religion." I stayed to listen anyway. I noticed that everyone seemed to represent different spiritual and religious backgrounds, yet it felt like they were all talking about the same thing. I heard someone reference the first five words in the book, "This is what I heard." That was a pivotal moment for me as I realized that none of us were face to face. We were all on an audible app listening to each other's voices. Moreover, we were all listening to the message that came through the book for each of us! The message would be heard differently based on each person's upbringing, education, beliefs, experiences, background, and conditioning.

Just like a diamond with various angles and sides, there would be various views about the same content--all reflecting back to us so that we could be introspective and consider it. I began to think that we are all here to reflect the divinity of that indescribable, inconceivable, presence that is always present. It's never in absence. It is always NOW HERE. Although we have given it all sorts of names like, I AM, God, Source, Christ-Consciousness, Buddhahood, All, Infinite Being and so on, we all *know* it because there is a resonance that happens deep within. We are all here and listening for what it seeks to express through us.

As I listened with my heart, what I heard began to cut away some of my old beliefs. Sometimes it would cut deep, and I had to sit and have honest talks with myself about old stories I'd held onto for years. Each person in the room represented a different angle of the diamond. Each person's share, attitude and expression caused me to see myself and consider why I perceived their views the way I did. Collectively, we all appeared as one, huge diamond.

I put some of my newly formed ideas into practice, and it felt like a sutra had sewn me up after bleeding out poisonous beliefs that were toxic to my well-being. Soon after, I decided to read *The Diamond Sutra* in the Ascension Community Club. That's when it dawned on me that to have a bartering community where everything worked harmoniously, where people happily gifted their talents to others without operating out of greed, or lack of integrity, it would require members of this community to ascend to an awareness that we are all here to reflect the divinity of "God".

We would all reach a point where we'd ask ourselves, *How is my life reflecting the divine nature within? How will this world be better because of my service?*

Each member would vibrate on a frequency that would not question, or have a need to question, anyone's intent. Each member would make the decision to do their own spiritual work. Each member would need to hear the message in the way they needed to hear it.

I created rules for the club that echoed this sentiment. In this club, there are no teachers except the one within each of us. Everyone in the room becomes a mirror and helps all our other selves to heal. The avatars we see on the app are just characters who came to play their roles and read their lines in each person's story. For my story, this is what I heard: because you chose, you are chosen.

While facilitating chat rooms in the Ascension Community, I face all types of challenges. As the creator, I have the greatest sense of accountability as I shoulder the responsibility to manage dialogue in the chat rooms and the integrity of the community as a whole. It feels like a big, bright light is always on me, but I know that I am no different than anyone else in the room. I, too, must do the work to awaken to the divinity within.

Choosing to surrender to your soul is saying, "Yes! I will walk in my purpose even when it is uncomfortable or unpopular."

As you begin to change habits and relationships that no longer serve your purpose, you'll find yourself surrounded by those who are on a similar journey and are in alignment with the person you have become. This is all a part of the transformation process, which has a beautiful view on the other side.

> "In this club, there are no teachers except the one within each of us."

My life continues to transform, and the Ascension Community remains a large part of the process. I've learned that it is important to keep our hearts open and to pose questions that highlight our service to others. I genuinely want to know, *How does my life serve others on this Earth? What lessons have I learned that I can share with someone else?*

I know that my life is being used to serve and, while in service to others, be served. This is the barter. When I am in this mode, I can express even more joy. This gives me greater human capacity; and the divine, through me, can express more of what it is. Because I chose, I understand that I will be presented with opportunities to address the ego/personality self, so that the soul can be revealed. I am here to re-present on Earth as it is in the mind of "God".

Choosing to surrender to my soul helped me realize that I am not the mere body, but rather the presence of God, the energy that flows through the body. This presence is what is thinking, hearing, and downloading the message to carry out its purpose here on Earth to the human me. I am willing to turn on the mute button to all the distractions so that I can hear the divine voice within.

A great awakening is occurring in the midst of narcissism, greed, mediocracy, and envy, but the chosen ones still press forward to build communities that are willing to rise up out of the shadows to speak to the possibility of a healed society where love and compassion is its foundation. I chose to step into the willingness to be great. I am not here to please people, but I am here to allow the soul to live out its purpose through me.

My story doesn't end. It is a constant unveiling of the divine. It is the inner-knowing and outer-growing that happens because I chose. My ascension journey has no ending. It comes with no manual or cheat sheet, yet my soul knows it all best. My ascension journey doesn't come with all the right moves. It just moves-- neither right, nor left. My ascension journey lets me know that because I chose, my potential is limitless.

I encourage every person who knows deep within that they received a divine vision to move forth in purpose and leadership--no matter who is with you or who is not. Allow what is within you to unlock, unleash, unveil and reveal itself fully through you. You are chosen.

LET'S CONNECT

https://www.LindaHooks.com
https://www.AscensionCommunity.org
PODCAST: *Anchor/LinLinSpeaks*

 TOOLS TO MINE YOUR DIAMOND

◆ 10-Second Rule: I began a 10-second rule where I trained myself to be mindful of how much time and energy I give to things that do not serve my well being or my life's purpose. If it doesn't make me feel good, then I won't give it more than 10 seconds of my time or attention. By putting a time limit on my interactions throughout the day, I more quickly realize when I am out of alignment with my divine nature.

◆ Mirror: I began to see everything as though it was holding up a mirror in front of me. Every person I encounter is simply another "myself". How I perceive others helps me to better identify what I need to work on in my own life. Everyone becomes my mirror. This mindset encourages me to go within to see what messages I need to pay attention to. Seeing others as I see myself is a beautiful way to practice compassion as well.

DISCUSSION QUESTIONS

Many are called, but few are chosen. Do you consider yourself one of the chosen few? If so, how will you stand strong when mediocracy challenges you as a leader?

How will people in this world become better individuals because of you?

REFLECT & RELEASE

REFLECT & RELEASE

THIS IS WHAT I HEARD

A MOMENT OF CLARITY

MELISSA CLAUDIO

Melissa Claudio is a mother of three girls: Alyse, Mya and Grace. She loves to spend time with the people she loves, and doing things she loves.
From reading, motivational speaking, writing, baking, creating content, helping others grow their business or speaking on public stages, Melissa puts love and intention into everything she does.

After years of depression, sadness, and feeling unworthy and like a waste of space, she was finally sick of her own shit and decided to make a change. Melissa is now an international best selling author and owner of Virtual Perfection, a freelance virtual assistant service agency. She is also the creator of the Daily Diamond Text Club, and works in book project management and author support services, as a writing coach, and is the creator of The Diamond Mine Literary Club.

Melissa's goal is to show people that no matter where you are in life right now, it doesn't have to stay that way. She decided to create the life of her dreams and wants to inspire others to do the same. *You are the captain of your ship, so you can adjust the sails and move accordingly,* she would say.

INSPIRATION

Infinite intelligence within me that knows all things, please divinely guide, protect and align me with all the people, places and things that are for my highest good. -- Melissa Claudio

First things first, if you are reading this, understand that there are no mistakes or coincidences in the universe. One thing I know for sure is that I wasn't looking for ascension, but it was definitely looking for me. When I asked what my purpose was in life and what I was actually meant to do here on earth, things changed. Unbeknownst to me, I was being guided by my inner knowing into a new chapter of life. I had always thought differently than other people and felt very alone. In my family, the term "black sheep" fit me like a glove throughout the years. I never felt a real connection with others but found a group of people who woke up my soul and changed the way I viewed the world. I learned that I wasn't weird; I was unique.

I took time over the past 3 years to really work on my life. I realized that no one could do it for me, and that life is the ultimate DIY job. As I learned more about myself, so many beautiful things started to pop up for me--opportunities that would eventually lead me to become an international best-selling author, and to do work in book project management and writing support services. Before all of that, life was very different.

Over the years, I've gone from depressed, overweight, anxious and miserable to healed, healthy and whole. I was sick of my own shit and ready to take control of my life. I decided to choose me.

In February 2021, I started a mindset bootcamp called 75 Hard by Andy Frisella. I was definitely intimidated by the idea of this challenge. I wasn't sure I'd complete it at first, but I would try anyway. It was a complete overhaul of the mind, and pushed me into terrain that enabled me to grow.

I started to wake up early, exercise twice a day, reading daily, writing affirmations, drinking a gallon of water a day, consumed no alcohol, bread, or added sugar. I have never kept a promise to myself--ever--but I completed the challenge. I was so proud because it was the first time I had done something for *me*.

> "I took time over the past 3 years to really work on my life. I realized that no one could do it for me, and that life is the ultimate DIY job."

As I showed up each day as my best self, I started to identify people who were also showing up as their best self. I discovered a social media platform called Clubhouse, and once I started to listen to the stories, I knew that I was learning things that could change my life. I took what I heard and implemented it into my daily life.

Showing up for myself and leading *me* first.

I added value to others without expectation. I had immense gratitude for everything, down to first morning breath. I refused to take things personally. I know I am not for everyone, and I am okay with it. I learned to embrace who I am as a person--my authentic self.

Once I stepped into my authentic self, people started to gravitate towards me. I wasn't chasing anymore; I was attracting more people like me by being me. Imagine that?

In August 2021, I came across the Ascension Community, and my life was never the same again. They were reading *The Diamond Sutra* and I happened to listen for a bit. To be honest, I didn't think I was smart enough to be in the room.

Listening to everyone speak about how they were impacted by the reading was life-changing. They were truly brilliant minds discussing truly beautiful things. Even though I was intimidated, I decided to go back in and listen again because I loved what I was hearing.

When we read chapters 11 and 12, there was something so profound about them that it brought me to tears. Knowing that I wasn't alone in the world and there were other beautiful souls out there was life-altering. I became aware that we are all one. Everyone is just another version of yourself. For the first time after seeing everyone else as amazing and majestic, I realized that it was already within me all along. It had never been more clear.

Being in this community with all of the amazing people I've met along the way has helped me *innerstand* that people are just reflections of each other. So, when I would say, "Wow, these people are amazing, smart, strong and beautiful!" It's because that's me! Someone told me once, "A butterfly never sees its wings." I saw myself in the wrong way for many years, but now I can finally see what everyone else sees.

I clearly remember how I felt the day that my awareness kicked in. I remember feeling like I was brand new. I needed to relearn myself and be grateful for where I am at all times. I saw the old version of myself completely transformed.

The Diamond Sutra showed me that I had to cut away the old versions of myself and let go of things that weighed me down to be the best version of myself.It also had the realization that we are all perfect, sacred, divine reflections of each other. Miracles. We are whole miracles. We are literal star dust. This changed the way I perceived my entire world.

As we read *The Diamond Sutra*, I awakened to my true divine self and met people who I know are my actual soul family. We may not be related, may not have grown up in the same house, same town or same states, but there is something bigger than us connecting us and bringing all of us together at this time. I stopped looking at myself as a separate *self* and see everyone as someone who brings value.

> "Knowing that I wasn't alone in the world
> and there were other beautiful souls out
> there was life-altering."

Everyone brings something different to the table, which makes things so beautiful because no one can do what you do--like you do. No one. You are the secret sauce. You are the original version.

After awakening to all of these beautiful truths, I started to look at life differently. I realized the importance of going within and really getting to know myself as a person. I became aware of things I used to take for granted, and now I give thanks daily. Now, I appreciate every breath I breathe because the next one is not guaranteed. Experiencing *The Diamond Sutra* changed everything for me, and for that I am forever grateful.

A few months later, in November of 2021, another book, *Frequency: The Power of Personal Vibration*, was to be read in the Ascension Community, so I decided to listen. I found myself reading and learning so much about myself.

The words that came off the pages of that book spoke to my soul. There were things I was already doing without knowing; and they were things that were a part of ascension and the inner healing work that accompanies it.

Most of what was spoken in the book were about self-reflection and healing. I was already reflecting daily but definitely had a lot of room to grow--especially when it came to issues of abandonment and self-worth.

I started to see why things were unfolding in my life the way they were. I got a true understanding of how to move in this world as someone who is incredibly unique. It led me to dive into healing family situations, and I decided it was time to leave the past in the past; because, technically, the only time is right now.

This very moment you are reading this is the only time. I learned it is a waste of your precious time to worry about things that happened in your life. Any pain, shame, guilt or misery that you feel about who you used to be should not hinder your growth. You can use the lessons you learn to help others. Regardless of what anyone else does, only you can control what you do. So, I continued to go within. If you're not growing, you're dying.

That being said, I do what is within my control. I show up for myself daily. I take care of myself. I reflect. I learn from the things I experience. I strive to be 1% better today than I was yesterday. I fill my cup daily. I know how to be the best version of myself and what it actually takes.

As we read *Frequency*, our discussions helped me to grow by leaps and bounds, and I decided I would share freely and authentically--no matter what. I saw that what I shared about my life and what I have endured helped others to navigate their lives more easily. It only takes one sentence to change someone's life forever.

Opening up and being authentic to share what I have learned on my journey is something I know I am here to do. I know my story can help others and inspire them to be their authentic self. I always wanted a space where I was free to share my experiences, good or bad. I discovered such a place with the Ascension Community, and it's forever changed my life.

This community has allowed me to be confident in knowing who I am. Just by authentically sharing my experiences I am able to help other people. I don't have to pretend to be someone I'm not; I no longer worry if people like me because I like me. I show up as myself and, if you are aligned, you will naturally gravitate to me without any resistance.

It's a beautiful thing. I get to share pain that I turned into my purpose to help others do the same. I knew a long time ago that I wasn't here to just be mediocre but I never knew anyone else who spoke the way I do. I didn't know anyone else who knew they were destined to do great things. I was divinely guided to align with others who also know they are here to do great things as well.

Over the past 6 months, I've experienced incredible growth. It started with taking accountability for myself and for where I was in life at the time. I decided where I wanted to grow from here. Yes, I said, *grow from here.*

I have had situations pop up in my everyday life that could have thrown me off track and made me stay in one place, but I know I wasn't put on this earth to suffer, and neither were you.

I've definitely grown in so many ways. I finally launched a project that I worked on for a while, but I didn't know exactly what I wanted to do with it.

> "Any pain, shame, guilt or misery that you feel about who you used to be should not hinder your growth. You can use the lessons you learn to help others."

I have gained more confidence over the last few months and was finally able to come into alignment with those who needed the services I could provide. Not only is it a perfect fit for me, I was able to ask for what I am truly worth. With this business up and running, I can grow and expand to help others with services and employ people as well.

Another project I launched helps people to write collaboratively in a book, or to write their own story. Building people up and leaving them better off than when I met them is absolutely priceless.

Bringing people together and building community with others is something I am very passionate about. I know that most people feel alone in their struggles. I also know that when others hear that they aren't alone in their struggles it makes it more bearable. Writing your story isn't just plopping words onto a page. It's sharing yourself with others, and being transparent and vulnerable that helps others to see that they are not alone.

Not only did rebuilding myself help me, it pours out onto those around me. By loving myself and showing up as my best self, I inspire others to do the same. Now, it's your turn to do it for yourself so that you can inspire others! Greatness is inside of you. Let it out and watch how quickly your world changes!

LET'S CONNECT

https://melissaclaudio.wixsite.com/virtualperfection-1
https://solo.to/themelissaclaudio
INSTAGRAM: @themelissaclaudio

THIS IS WHAT I HEARD

 # TOOLS TO MINE YOUR DIAMOND

- ◈ There were various things that helped me get through rough patches along my journey. Staying consistent with my daily affirmations was key for me. Affirmations allowed me to create a new narrative for myself. I used the affirmations to reprogram the lack, shame and guilt I experienced. It is daily work and not a "once in a while" thing.

- ◈ Staying aligned with people who has similar mindsets is also beneficial. I look to be around people who have a miracle mindset--those who expect miracles and good things in their life. I am able to align with people who are of my highest good because I show up as the best version of myself daily. When I made myself whole, I attracted other people who were also whole.

....

 # DISCUSSION QUESTIONS

What is something you can do to show yourself grace?

What would the most healed, happiest, whole version of you look like?

REFLECT & RELEASE

REFLECT & RELEASE

THIS IS WHAT I HEARD

THE "IN" GAME

TANGENIQUE KING

Tangenique is a California native from San Francisco. She is a mother of four: Au'Zhonii (25), Aziyah (18), Astauzyah (6) and Ah'Seer (5); and one granddaughter, Majestii.

From an early age, Tangenique has been an exceptional artist, designer and hairstylist. She has spent over 20 years in the beauty industry, owns her own salons and is involved in many hair shows. Tangenique connects deeply with others through her passionate views of beauty and loves to make people look and feel their best. She has the ability to find loveliness in many things, which includes home decor and apparel design. Through her art, she creates from her heart. Tangenique is heavily involved in a social media platform called the Ascension Community on Clubhouse that expresses the importance of inner work which leads one on their ascension path to greatness--one step at a time. Her mission is to reach many by being herself, through complete transparency, love and integrity. It is her endeavor to make sure that she offers the best version of herself and is a beacon of light that shows others the way within.

INSPIRATION

I AM.
-- Tangenique King

The journey within has indeed been a highly transitional one to say the least. This road by far has been long and filled with ups and downs, laughter and sorrow; but the one thing about it is that it is my own. It is my own to explore and evaluate and not to live through someone else's eyes.

I spent a very long time living for others and exhausting myself to show people how genuine I am, and how loving and forgiving I could be at any cost. I primarily did this for my mother. Don't get me wrong, I loved her with all of my heart, and I know she loved me. However, certain choices she made caused me to not have much of a childhood. I prematurely had the responsibility of taking care of my younger siblings. My beautiful mommy suffered from decades of substance abuse and would leave her children in desolate dispositions more times than not. Regardless, I stuck in there with her and would do anything for her.

I had been her co-dependent from the age of seven until well into my thirties. It was heart-wrenching from day to day. I wouldn't wish missing out on a quality, love and fun-filled childhood on anyone. I literally put my siblings' needs over my own all the time. It stunted my growth tremendously, and the inability to develop properly is mentally draining.

Life always seemed unfair. I freely gave every part myself, which eventually led me down a path of self-destruction and disillusionment. It made me feel unworthy of any possibility of greatness. I didn't matter. I couldn't know what it would even feel like to matter. I couldn't see the forest for the trees and I didn't envision myself creating a life beyond the environment I had been subjected to throughout those adolescent years. I hadn't a clue that all I had to do was show up for myself and unapologetically love myself from inside!

That mindset, and especially the concept of "being", didn't exist by a long shot in my eyes. Today, I am so grateful to awake in this reality with a new outlook on life. I can finally see the big picture with purpose, and I know that none of my experiences have been in vain! Though it all seemed like an uphill battle filled with uncertainty and void of healthy confidence, somehow I managed to press forward. I decided that I would not walk in anyone's shadow, and it turns out that I was walking in my own shadow.

A new sheriff was on the scene. I have always been a very intuitive person, and I also prided myself on having a keen ear and vision for the spiritual realm. I strongly believe this gift has kept me out of harm's way in many situations. As a young adult, I spent a major amount of time studying different religions even though I had a strong background in Christianity. For some reason, my favorite was Buddhism. I was introduced to it by a friend of mine and her mother. Their lives seemed to flow despite certain mishaps that would occur. Still, I somehow felt that something was missing from my spiritual connection.

One day, I found myself. It didn't matter how much I studied, it all led me to the same conclusion. I started to question where all of my discoveries were truly leading me. My quest seemed to only lead to dead ends; all I had was knowledge and no true direction.

Nothing could seem to compare to the longing I had for what was calling out to me from deep within myself. I had many dreams that displayed a greater version of me, but I didn't know the first step to start the process of finding her. To my surprise, the version of me that I often dreamed was actually part of my original blueprint. I had this unshakable desire to unlock the shackles of my darkness. It seemed as though the stars had aligned on my behalf when I began the quest to find the **real** me.

My sister called me one day out of the blue and told me about this app called Clubhouse. I seldom indulge in social media, so I looked at her sideways--through the phone, of course. I was very apprehensive. The bigger part of me is a straight up hermit, but I felt the need to take a chance without knowing what to expect. I heard Source tell me that I needed to exercise my throat chakra and be where the creators are. It would all take place on Clubhouse.

> "I had many dreams that displayed a greater version of me, but I didn't know the first step to start the process of finding her."

I entered a room that my sister was entertaining at the time. After a few weeks in there, I gained a good rapport with the people. When it started to get wild, I moved into a room that would help with my relationship with money. I didn't realize I had resentment towards money, and the root of that resentment was brought to my awareness. I slowly but surely gained momentum in these Clubhouse streets and was breaking down walls within myself like "Tetris".

I met an awesome lady in the room where I first started who was an author, and we communicated often in pursuit of starting a podcast together. She was also working with a group of ladies who were conducting a room called "Diamond Sutra". Since I had some familiarity with Buddhism, the thought of this room resonated with me.

In this particular room, they were reading *The Diamond Sutra* in cycles. The reading had thirty two chapters and the group would start again after those were complete. In this room, I met LinLin, and she was hearing *The Diamond Sutra* for the first time as well. We would all read and have discussions after each chapter. We would share according to how we heard the chapter. Soon, it was time for a new round. I volunteered and so did Lin, which led us to co-moderating. From that point, we kept going with the readings, and I could feel it changing my life.

When it was time for another round, Lin decided to do it in a club she created that she called the Ascension Community. She had developed it based on a vision she had before entering the Clubhouse platform. Her mission was intriguing and in alignment with my purpose, so I decided to accompany her in the next round. I was so excited to join her and experience this community from its foundation. It would be the third round for me, but would take place in the Ascension Community. It was such a monumental moment.

> "From that point, we kept going with the readings, and I could feel it changing my life."

I had stepped into my star power! I was actually doing what I set out to do, which is to let the world know that I have a voice, and that voice will be used to uplift others as I rise in self-actualization.

In the Ascension Community, I could see a genuineness developing like no other and I was so elated to be a part of something so beautiful. It is a space for people like me to share my unorthodox explanations of what I see in my visions from the unseen. It is a place of healing for someone who grew up like me. I have vivid dreams, and I am finally able to share them with others in a safe space.

In the community, I hear reflections that strike the very core of my being. The transparency is undeniable. I feel myself grow stronger and stronger everyday. The best part is that people can be themselves without having to play small. I have been stretched in so many directions and I feel like I'm 20 feet tall!

I have bossed up tremendously. I assist with moderating this space, and we have read books that literally shovel out old constructs that have lain dormant inside of us for the longest. I can't help but to believe that the Most High would see fit to design such a marvelous place to spend my precious time.

You see, this is what I heard: *Go to where the creators are.* Lo and behold, as I went, a place was simultaneously being created for me and others like me to expand. It reminds me of the ten lepers who went into Jerusalem, and *as they went* they were healed because they answered the call from within. As I move forward, I am healed because I too answer the call, which, for me, is a feeling of urgency. I started to realize that the way I used to do things didn't work any longer. After being agitated about it, I began to sit with myself for a change.

It was the most awkward thing I've ever done because I was used to ignoring myself and tending to others. It felt foreign because it was. I was a foreigner in my own home--in my own being. How sad is it to not *see* the person I'm with everyday?

I stand here today and say that if all you hear is, "Don't give up," please listen. I never thought that I would have so much clarity after coming out of the illusion that I was in complete darkness. When I stepped into the light, I realized that it was actually me in the spotlight. The only fact was that I hadn't yet taken my place on stage. That was it! The reward is genuine beauty and uniqueness. A divine being is waiting to embrace you with open arms. What awaits is the *you* that you have always been--the original you, the one that truly loves you. I promise you won't have to look any further. Your search will be over.

LET'S CONNECT

www.AscensionCommunity.org
INSTAGRAM: *@crownedchakra*
CLUBHOUSE: *@TangeniqueTalana*

THIS IS WHAT I HEARD

TOOLS TO MINE YOUR DIAMOND

- 💎 Be kind to yourself. It took a long time to get to where you are, and it will take no time to get to where you're going! Inward and upward!

- 💎 Realize that alignment is the equivalent to meditation. Be still enough to have a listening ear for your true identity. It's an inside job!

....

DISCUSSION QUESTIONS

In your quiet place, what can you hear calling out to you from the depths of your soul that's leading you to connect with your higher self?

What attributes do you acquire that would be a catalyst to activate your journey to ascension?

REFLECT & RELEASE

📝 REFLECT & RELEASE

THIS IS WHAT I HEARD

JOURNEYING BACK TO THE SELF

NINA CURTIS

Nina has worked over a decade in the technology sector. After a spiritual awakening in 2020, Nina felt called to be of service to those in their transformational journey just as others had done throughout her personal journey. Nina now partners with others as a Transformation and Recovery Coach, sacred space holder, and facilitator of breath work. In this lifetime, Nina has taken on the role of mom, advocate for autism, and continued study of the human condition. Nina's hobbies and interests include learning the esoteric sciences, philosophy, community engagement, connecting with nature, feminine embodiment practices and the study of plants and herbs. Nina is an avid researcher and has taken an interest in learning how the ancient spiritual practice of entheogenic use can assist others on their path to healing and ascension. Nina's mission is to continually brighten her light to remind others of the light that is already within them.

INSPIRATION

Above all else, I want to see things differently. God is in everything I see. I could see peace instead of this.
—- A Course in Miracles

In 2020 BC (before COVID), life was beginning to feel like a never-ending struggle. I was a 41-year-old woman who felt overwhelmed by the daily demands of life. I was in a marriage at that time, but it felt as though I was a single parent raising a child with unique needs. I remember feeling like I was trapped in an infinite loop of the same repetitive actions each and every day. Each morning, I'd struggle with getting my anxiety-filled child motivated to go to school. My school drop-off/pick-up and work/home commute was about one and half hours each way. In addition, my evenings were filled with doctors appointments, therapies, and extracurricular activities. My husband at the time was married to his work and didn't have the emotional bandwidth to assist me with the daily physical and emotional tasks required to raise a neuro divergent child. I felt incredibly alone, like I was dying a slow, lonely, numbing death. I was lost and I didn't know who I was anymore.

One morning, in the rush to leave the house during our normal daily routine, I hit the garage as I pulled out of the driveway. It was a defining *a-ha* moment for me. I was so busy in the rush of *doing*, or trying to get somewhere, that I was running on autopilot and was no longer present. I was running an unconscious program. I paused and considered that the outcome may have been far worse under a different set of circumstances. What if I were on the highway as opposed to my driveway and was involved in a tragic collision that harmed both myself and my child? I knew that something needed to change; but I didn't know how to escape this repetitive loop of "doing" that had me trapped.

Amid these experiences, COVID-19 forced the world into lockdown. Work and school had gone remote. Doctors appointments and therapies were either canceled or virtual. I suddenly had three or more additional hours in my day that I didn't have prior to 2020 BC. I made the conscious decision to use the time mindfully and reacclimated myself to practicing transcendental meditation for an hour to an hour and a half each day.

Not too long after the lockdowns and re-incorporating meditation into my routine did I start to experience energetic and awareness shifts along with many synchronicities. It all led to an opportunity to attend a spiritual retreat. When it was presented to me, my body vibrated with an excited, energetic *yes*. I couldn't explain it at the time, but I knew my higher self was guiding me this experience. Looking back, I'm grateful to have became still enough to listen to my inner voice long enough to hear. It was the exact experience I would need at that point in my soul's journey to reconnect with myself. The weekend-long retreat was transformational.

> "I was so busy in the rush of doing, or trying to get somewhere, that I was running on autopilot and was no longer present. I was running an unconscious program."

I returned from the retreat a different person. I was no longer numb. I could feel every single emotion that I had abandoned through the years--bliss, joy, love, sadness, grief, and gratitude. It had been so long since I had experienced this spectrum of feelings. My kundalini had awakened and I was happy to be aware that I was in the driver's seat and could choose to steer the next adventure in my journey wherever I wanted to go. I made a personal vow to never allow myself to be a passenger stuck on autopilot in my life again.

After such a profound experience and with a new passion for life, I knew it was time to seek a community of like-minded individuals and safe containers to continue the unfolding of my awakening and feel supported. I found community with other retreat participants through weekly Zoom integration sessions. However, I realized it was time to spread my wings, expand outside of that container and connect with others. The challenge I encountered was that the world was still shut down and opportunities for connecting and meeting new people were limited. Towards the end of 2020, I was invited to a new social networking audio app, Clubhouse, which is where I was introduced to the Ascension Community Club.

When I "dropped in" to the Ascension Community, they were doing a live reading of a book that I was also reading and integrating on my own, *Conversations with God* by Neale Donald Walsh. The dialogue surrounding the book's content was profound. *Here is a group of like-minded individuals all doing the internal work to elevate themselves,* I thought to myself. They were welcoming, spiritual seekers, working on personal development and reading the same book that I had also been reading. I was filled with gratitude that there was a group setting where I could discuss this book and better integrate my discoveries.

THIS IS WHAT I HEARD

I joined the members of the Ascension Community Club to read and discuss a chapter of the *The Diamond Sutra* each weekday. One of the first things I noticed about this community is that it is a container for everyone no matter where we are in our spiritual journeys. It was not a club with guru's or teachers. In fact, the club's leaders often emphasize that "there are no teachers here" and will instead direct those that come into the room to go inward and speak to "what they heard" in any given passage that's been read.

What is so beautiful about the container is witnessing different perspectives that arise from each individual through their shares of what comes up for them. I witness many synchronicities. One individual's share may be exactly what another individual needed to hear at that moment. Another's share may help someone understand a worldview they hadn't considered before. Profound shifts were happening for many in the room-- myself included. Absolutely beautiful! I've witnessed the process of quantum entanglement in action.

Synchronicities that I experienced included being introduced to book readings that explained some of the shifts I was experiencing in my personal life. I also noticed that some of the room titles corresponded to repetitive number sequences on the dates that the room was hosted (i.e. 333 on 12-12-21 and 222 on 2-22-22) and wasn't done intentionally by the club's hosts.

While this may appear coincidental, I realized that I connect with my Higher Self through numbers and sequences; therefore, I process these occurrences as little nods from the universe. In addition, a concept that would have been shared in the room would come up in another conversation the same day outside of the room; or I'd happen to watch a movie that would tie together something that was presented in the Ascension Community that I was in the process of integrating.

> "Here is a group of like-minded individuals all doing the internal work to elevate themselves..."

What I heard that impacted me most in the Ascension Community is: *There is only one of us here*. This statement is repeated by one of the club leaders frequently, but it is possibly the statement that sticks with me most. It serves as a reminder that there is, in fact, no separation, and that what I see in another is merely a projection of what is within myself. If someone triggers something within me, they are showing up in that moment as a teacher to lovingly identify what is being brought to the surface and should be addressed. They are but a reflection for me to fully see myself. If I see something that is admirable in another, they too are a reflection of the light that is within me. They are me and I am them. This statement reinforced in me what I already knew to be true--that we are all one human body, a divine extension of The All, expressing ourselves as individuals. There is truly only one of us here. It really is that simple.

Since coming into the Ascension Community, my life has transformed in a variety of ways. I've become much more confident when I vulnerably speak in public and amongst groups, which I credit to the safe container that has been created by the club's leaders.

Within the club, each person's share is just as important as the next. Each individual is encouraged to share their unique perspective, which is not only to their benefit, but a benefit to the entire community. Through hearing everyone's shares, I've learned that we are all just--in the words of Ram Dass--*walking each other home*. I do not experience the complexities of the human condition on an island by myself. We are all on a soul's journey, and through our individual human experiences, we are finding our way back home to ourselves.

> "If someone triggers something within me, they are showing up in that moment as a teacher to lovingly identify what is being brought to the surface and should be addressed."

Witnessing the transformation of others is encouraging. For example, a member has become a best selling book author since joining the community. Through witnessing this individual's journey, I've felt inspired to share my story through writing in hopes that it may be as much of an inspiration for others as their stories are for me. I have built the confidence to host rooms in Clubhouse and introduce books that were pivotal to my growth, which is something I would never have considered prior to coming into this community.

By speaking in clubhouse rooms, I've built connections with interesting people from all over the world, and many have become friends and business partners.

The journey back to myself began at the time of my birth, but my awakening happened in 2020, when I made time to get still and hear the voice of infinite wisdom, my higher self. The world around me didn't change, but my awareness of the world did. I began to see what my eyes could not see before, and hear what I had been unable to hear in times prior. I began to follow the breadcrumbs and pay attention to the synchronicities that were showing up. I was led to the Ascension Community, which led to developing new relationships--both personal and professional.

I've stepped out of my comfort zone to do things that I would have never before considered. You're now reading the words of a published author. How about that! I no longer feel like a victim of circumstances. I feel like my life is a movie and I am the script writer, the antagonist, the protagonist, the director, the lead, and all of the supporting roles. I'm in the process of writing a new movie for the brand new me.

This improvement came about by becoming still and going within. I am no different from you. Whatever you can imagine for yourself, you can create. After all, there is only one of us here. No matter your past circumstances, you can become the hero of your own journey. I've returned home to my true self, and it feels so good to be back.

LET'S CONNECT

www.youralchemycoach.com
YOUTUBE: *The Alchemical Container*
PODCAST: *The Alchemical Container*

THIS IS WHAT I HEARD

 # TOOLS TO MINE YOUR DIAMOND

- ◇ Make time for stillness. One cannot hear the voice of Higher Wisdom if you are consumed with busyness and distractions. In our fast world of social media, streaming services, work and responsibilities, it's easy to fill the mind with voices and information that isn't yours. Our natural essence is to be, which is why we are human beings. The answers are always within and are found in the stillness.

- ◇ Community is medicine. Finding a safe container of like minded individuals who are working on themselves can help to support you in your ascension journey. The path of spiritual awakening does not come without its challenges. One may find that they no longer relate to the communities they were once a part of prior to their awakening and may feel alone and without support for the next level of their process. Being safely held and witnessed by others in the journey is medicine.

 # DISCUSSION QUESTIONS

What are three acts of self care that you can practice to honor yourself each day?

THIS IS WHAT I HEARD

Life is always happening for you, not to you. In what ways can you change your perspective in a challenging situation you are facing to see the gift in the experience?

REFLECT & RELEASE

REFLECT & RELEASE

THIS IS WHAT I HEARD

SEEING THE WOOD FOR THE TREES

RACHAEL EBANKS-GOLD

Rachael is a coach and registered dietitian. She combines nutrition and mindfulness with one-to-one coaching to help her clients achieve their life and wellness goals.

Devoted to personal growth, she uses her own challenges as inspiration to help others. Rachael firmly believes that underneath daily internal and external stresses lies the healthiest, happiest, kindest, and most abundant versions of ourselves--no matter what the inner critic would have us believe.

Her mission is to continue to expand and help others to develop their awareness, see past mental limitations and step into the person they've always been at their core. She is also passionate about animal rights, sustainable living, and removing the stigma around mental health issues.

Rachael was born and raised in London, United Kingdom, and is the youngest of five children. She currently works virtually and lives in Europe with her partner and cats. She's fanatical about tea and loves to hike in nature and create delicious vegetarian recipes. In the future, she plans to adopt more animals, lead wellness retreats and create life-changing workshops.

INSPIRATION

You are all that you need to be. -- Rachael Ebanks-Gold

I've always felt connected to something beyond me. Since I was a child, whenever I looked up at the night sky, I could feel this gap between what my worldly self knew and the fullness of what I was actually a part of. This sense of wonder and belonging was influenced by my childhood involvement in Christianity, the mindfulness practice I had discovered in my twenties, and also the movie, *The Secret*.

Yet, like many people, my identity was stained by beliefs that I wasn't good enough and that I didn't belong. Spirituality, for me, took the form of a relationship between an aspect of myself who was wise, strong, and determined and the other part who was weaker and needier. It was very much a parent-child dynamic--warm, comforting, and full of dependency.

My spiritual beliefs and practices meant that I could bounce back from emotional challenges, quiet my mind when it went down the wrong road, and gather profoundly helpful insights through long journaling sessions. I'd even see "signs" that something out there was rooting for me. The perfect message would land in my inbox moments before I had to make a tough decision. Clients emerged from thin air at just the right time. Dreams at night hinted at events that would occur the following morning.

Despite my belief and awareness, I was still stunted by my notions of being alone and insufficient. Spirituality wasn't power; it was a way to soothe myself because the world was painful to me. This deep sense of insecurity caused me to hold back.

New friendships weren't given time to bloom. I'd let work opportunities pass over to the person next to me--who I assumed must be better in some way. I'd be excited by new, creative ideas, and then give up with a sense of hopelessness before I would give myself a chance to plant the first seed. And to top it off, the voice of imposter syndrome would step in and judge my self-judgment: *You know, you can't help people if you're struggling yourself.*

It felt like a blessing when I came across the Ascension Community. At the time, I'd been working for myself for a few months and was feeling overwhelmed and anxious. There were so many things to be done, and so many things that I wanted to create; but my progress was blocked by self-doubt and procrastination. Of course, I made a conscious effort to refocus my attention toward positive thoughts. However, it was hard, and I would only get so far. After all, I was still holding this limited perception that the world was unsafe and I was insufficient. I was subconsciously trying to figure out how to become *good enough*.

One afternoon around this difficult time, I was scrolling through the Clubhouse app. Angel numbers--the same number repeated three or four times--tend to catch my attention. So, when I saw the title, "Frequency 333", I immediately clicked on it to enter the virtual room (the space where a specific conversation is held on the app).

> "There were so many things to be done, and so many things that I wanted to create; but my progress was blocked by self-doubt and procrastination."

Usually, I flit impatiently in and out of rooms, but this time I stopped to listen with my full attention. It had a very nurturing vibe. The group was discussing the book, *Frequency*, by Penney Peirce. I was curious because I'd heard the word "frequency", along with "energy" and "vibrations", used in spiritual circles before. I had my own sense of their meaning but it was very vague.

As I listened in, I got the feeling that I was meant to be in this space. In fact, I fully believe that some force had aligned me with it. I can't remember what was said on that first day, but I remember how I felt. I was safe, stimulated, alive, and not alone! I also had an exciting sense that answers were on their way to me.

Two or three hours passed before I clicked the "leave quietly" button and put my phone down. As I made a cup of tea, I smiled to myself. I felt warmer and lighter. It was as though, in an instant, the contents of my worried thoughts didn't matter anymore.

Needless to say, I joined the community and returned almost daily to listen while preparing my lunch. Several months have passed now, and I've received many gems that have altered how I think and feel. The first big message I received was that despite having a physical form, I'm not just one person in a physical body. The energy within me is the same energy in everyone and everything else; there's no separation.

I had to feel this to really understand it. And I did so by bringing awareness to the sensations of my vibrating cells and by tuning in to the feeling of the energy directly around me, above me, and even in my cat!

It's so subtle, but the more I tune in with intention, the more I can sense it. It's like a direct connection between my physical self and my higher self, and everything and everyone else.

> "The energy within me is the same energy in everyone and everything else; there's no separation."

Through this awareness, I've become more of a *feeler* and less of a *thinker*. When I feel through my day, as opposed to thinking through it, my sense of self expands automatically. For example, when I'm driving, I'm not alone. I am the whole experience: the person driving the car, the other cars, the trees, the pedestrians, the sky. When I feel into my experience like this--free of categorizing and personal storytelling--there's a lightness to life that was so rare before. I become larger and less solid, which releases the pressure of any anxious, me-centric thoughts. I realize that I don't need to control things or try to be anything. I don't need to *improve* or live up to anyone's expectations. Nor do I need to put all my human parts in perfect order to feel like I'm good enough. Newsflash Rachael: you're not here to be perfect! I'm here to experience and to grow and to help others grow.

This insight was compounded by another message I received while in the group: I can't grow and be small at the same time. The belief that I needed to protect myself from the harsh, judgmental world was exactly what caused me the most pain. I had a choice to make. Option one: safety, comfort, hiding and feeling stuck. Or, option two: growth, discomfort, being seen, feeling more connected.

Clearly, option two is my only option, I thought. Damn. It felt frightening and liberating all at once. How do I take the leap? I journaled on it. What I needed was to practice trust. I must trust that whatever I need to be or experience is exactly what I will be or experience; trust that I am supported and loved; trust that the more I let go of the need to control, the higher I go.

Truly embedding trust would mean that when I start a creative project with excitement and then suddenly hit a wall of uncertainty, it's okay. Instead of going straight to, "You're terrible at this, stop now!" I can take a moment to readjust, and then keep going.

Trust would also mean that instead of muzzling myself when I have something to say, I remember that my message came from my soul, and therefore needs to be expressed.

> "I don't need to improve or live up to anyone's expectations. Nor do I need to put all my human parts in perfect order to feel like I'm good enough."

This clarity felt so empowering, yet the impact wasn't quite enough for me to break free from myself. For example, on several occasions when I was in Ascension Community rooms, I would feel a rush of insight that wanted to be shared, but I would stop myself. I'd force myself to think long and hard about what I was going to say, and as I did this, the energy of the insight faded. Only fear remained, so I'd keep quiet. It was horrible. I felt so moronic and encaged. I was frustrated that I hadn't integrated my wisdom enough to create new habits.

THIS IS WHAT I HEARD

I asked the Universe: *What do I need to know or experience in order to fully let myself be?*

The following night, while using a meditation app, I stumbled across an audio of lesson 65-66 of *A Course In Miracles*. Nothing is coincidental, so I listened deeply. The gist of the message was: My only function is the one God gave me. My happiness and my function are one.

This spoke volumes. By committing to my deep desire to be of service to others, I can cut through all the fear and worries in regards to my Self. Who cares if my words are perfect if I'm expressing truth? My function isn't to speak perfectly. Who cares about rejection? My function isn't to be loved by everyone.

Life suddenly seemed a lot simpler. The next day, despite my body being tense with resistance and cortisol, I voluntarily shared my thoughts with the community for the first time ever. It felt like a victory.

Of course, daily life and the nature of the mind will continue to provide us with many opportunities to get sucked back into the illusion of separation, solidity and smallness. However, I don't dwell in dark places for very long anymore. This is thanks to another message I received in the Ascension Community--that my higher self is always guiding me toward growth and, ultimately, freedom and joy.

I've always felt guided, but in the past it was only in "happy luck" situations. I now see that the not-so-pleasant parts of life aren't the punishments they can feel like. They're actually a doorway to the next level.

I see wise messages and meaning in everything. For example, a period of inconsistent income became an opportunity to see that I can live well on less than I thought, and I became aware of all the previously under-appreciated ways that proved I was indeed rich. I live in a safe country. I have food in the fridge. I have total freedom in regards to my time and flexibility, high-speed internet and near-perfect health. When I moved to a new place with my partner and found that I didn't like the local area, it created an opportunity to build the skill of equanimity. I had to learn to unconditionally be completely at peace, and to be okay inside regardless of what existed outside. Having a constant flow of income, or living in the perfect place wouldn't have allowed me to create this level of emotional independence.

Even having my laptop and phone crash one after the other on the same day has been helpful. As I was forced to take a pause, I noticed that my body was tense and my energy was low. I realized that, just as it was with the electronic devices, forcing myself to overwork would only lead to a breakdown.

> "I became aware of all the previously under-appreciated ways that proved I was indeed rich."

Problems aren't solid things to struggle with, people. They're lines of inquiry. Instead of resisting and feeling stuck--as if life is happening *to* us--we can use curiosity to create movement, and eventually see how life is happening *for* us.

The realizations that I am bigger than my worldly self, that there are no real problems, and that I am always being guided towards growth and freedom, have been an immense relief and source of strength.

I used to judge myself for having "issues", but as I trust that I am exactly how I am meant to be, I now see the wood for the trees. I see that my issues are just as much jewels as the parts of me that are culturally perceived as good. I see that I am not alone, and the world isn't so scary. I see that my pain is the same pain that every being on this planet feels. And now, I'm even more determined than before to be part of the solution.

I used to meditate to unhook from thoughts and to wrap myself up in the comfort of the present moment, but was still firmly locked in the myth of separation. Now, I meditate to reconnect to the physical and non-physical parts of me, and beyond. Rather than being a tool for self-protection, meditation is a reminder that there is nothing from which I would need to protect myself.

With that all said, at times, heightened spiritual awareness can feel like an unwanted responsibility. It's become more obvious when I engage with some small habit of mind and when there's an opening or a request for me to step up. I can't revert to the old curling up into a ball mode anymore. I'm beyond that; and I have to act like it. Talk about pressure! When you know what your soul wants, you see that in listening to it, there is zero possibility of losing. Therefore, discomfort must be welcomed, and I can take small steps in that regard.

On the outside, my life hasn't changed dramatically, but I feel greatly supported. My once scared heart is beginning to flutter open, and the goal is neither perfection nor protection--and that's a huge relief.

I have fully committed to remembering that I am more than me, to listening to what my soul wants, and to allowing myself to unfold completely. It certainly won't be a smooth road, and my ego will try to resist my growth; but I trust that, for all of us, there's no better way.

LET'S CONNECT

Book Recommendation: *Radical Compassion* **by Tara Brach**
YOUTUBE: *Rachael Ebanks-Gold*
INSTAGRAM: *@rachaelebanksgold*

TOOLS TO MINE YOUR DIAMOND

◇ First things first, let difficult emotions be felt. If you ignore them, they'll only come back. In her book <u>Instant Cosmic Ordering</u>, Barbel Mohr writes, "Each feeling contains its opposite when felt to its fullest extent." So, resist the urge to push negative emotions aside. Feel the low, and you will get to the high.

Observe how the emotion is showing up in your experience. For example, notice where the feeling of sadness is located in your body, and identify physical sensations attached to it. You can also release your emotions through crying, talking it out with someone that makes you feel safe, or journaling.

- Self-compassion is also key. Our tendency to be hard on ourselves can be amplified as we become more aware since we may notice more things about ourselves that we want to change. Beware! Self-criticism only causes more stress and blocks our ability to think clearly.

When you notice self-judgmental thoughts that don't feel good, consciously unhook from them. Remember that we all struggle, and that change is not a linear process. Wherever you are now, it's at least one step ahead of where you were before! Try placing a hand on your heart as a gesture of kindness and understanding. Appreciate yourself; you're doing the best you can, and that is enough.

DISCUSSION QUESTIONS

Think about an unpleasant aspect of your current circumstances. Observe your thoughts and feelings without getting sucked too deep into the storyline.

Ask yourself: What value does this have? What point does my soul or higher self want me to get to by having this experience?

In what ways are you being overly protective yourself? How is this stunting your growth and expansion? What would happen if you were to fully let go?

✎ REFLECT & RELEASE

REFLECT & RELEASE

THIS IS WHAT I HEARD

I EXIST AS WE, WE EXIST AS I

KIMBERLY GARDNER, PH.D.

Kimberly Gardner is a native of Atlanta, Georgia and holds a doctorate of philosophy in mathematics teaching and learning. She is a wife, mother, and mathematics educator with over thirty years of experience at the secondary and tertiary levels. She has helped countless youth and young adults achieve in school through mentorship and academic advising. Throughout her career, she has received awards for outstanding teaching and service to her school, and has published works on interdisciplinary approaches to teaching science, technology, engineering and mathematics to marginalized students. Kimberly is also an instructor of beginner's Qigong and Tai Chi, and teaches in various parks in her community to promote well-being for all. Quite the introvert, she does not boast a significant social media or virtual presence, but she has aspirations to begin streaming content for her various interests in the near future.

INSPIRATION

Let love and peace rule your heart and seek spiritual serendipity in all things. -- Kimberly Gardner, Ph.D.

One late autumn morning in 2021 during the COVID-19 pandemic, I was on my back porch sipping a cup of herbal tea when I was pinged by LinLin, the founder and moderator of the Ascension Community, as she hosted a room on the Clubhouse app. The discussion was on a passage from the book, *Frequency*, by Penney Peirce. Upon entering the room, I heard, "I am because you are. I exist because you exist," spoken by a brother I later learned goes by the name Calvin. His words flowed into my heart like the rap sessions of community elders from my youth.

I was transported back to a time when the parables of the day were about elevation of mind, rising above oppression while paying homage to the struggle, and raising Black consciousness through awareness of our ancient lost legacies as the originators of civilization. A time when sacred knowledge and spiritual laws were transmitted through the storytelling of our ancient genealogy, these oral histories were a mechanism for ascension.

I quickly realized that while his essence spoke inspiration from the past, we were presently experiencing a cataclysm. Death, grief and loss on every doorstep was the insidious greeting of the pandemic. It also deepened and exposed raw, unhealed "-isms" such that the re-centering of the unity curve significantly shifted, which put its tail at skewness and disunity. The gross asymmetry gave rise to low-frequency mind to action manifestations experienced globally through racial unrest, food and housing insecurity, extensive widening of the wealth gap and astronomical increases in mental health crises--just to name a few unresolved injustices humankind chose to ignore prior to the moment. The pandemic focused them simultaneously in the same lens, and exposed truths we all had no choice but to examine.

As I listened to other shares during the discussion, I recalled the tingling of my metaphysical senses during the initial global shutdown and quarantine. In 2020, I was still grieving the 2019 transition of my "World's Best Dad", and I agonized over the bitter contentiousness and depression of a troubled marriage. Either one of these life growth spurts alone would have been stressful enough, but both occurring at the same time coupled with global uncertainty about everything were mentally, physically and metaphysically traumatic. I sensed that the cosmos was clutching everything I thought was stable and real into a fist, crumpling it all into one unidentifiable mass and casting it into a putrid decaying trash heap.

> "I quickly realized that while his essence spoke inspiration from the past, we were presently experiencing a cataclysm."

What I thought was real, the institutions I thought were stable, the people and sources I thought credible, the race and gender equity progress I thought the country and world had made were all dissolving, the delusion concluding. Yet I still existed, we still existed in the aftermath of our own bite from the fruit of Eden's tree, the Tree of the Knowledge of Good and Evil. I felt as if my spirit was done with having this human experience, but my humanness needed my spirit to step up and save us. I felt the brutal duel between my spiritual and physical self. My body maintained its life force but, without proximity to spirit, it was like a mindless animated meat mass. The disharmony and malcontent between them plunged us into a pit of misery.

A distress signal from my internal light pulsated multidimensionally through the cosmos to The First Responder; the Creator rescued me. The transmission to my spirit was to detach my life chords from useless earthly things that anchored me to this realm and then I heard: *follow ME*. I surrendered. I spiritually invoked breaking the chains of my anchors, and followed. I sought the Divine with all my heart, mind, spirit and might, but with a much different mindset from my previous 52 years on this planet. I severed ties with all things that did not serve me spiritually. People, unhealthy food and beverage, lack of fitness, mainstream media, social media, music, the internet, television and radio were all disconnected. In the silence, I experienced bliss; and through baptism in light and angelic sound, I was reborn. After my physical and spiritual purges, one by one people and things bearing light began to find me and I also sought and found them.

Immersed in simplicity and peace of a quiet mind, the thought "I AM" presented itself and I acknowledged that I existed. In the absence of my familiar, and in my now dismantled and purged concept of reality, I was only permitted a view of the collective *we as me*. With all my comfortable and familiar distractions stripped away and bringing just us into view, I questioned what was real. I heard Spirit answer, *You, I, and We are One.* A thought floated a paraphrase from the poet, Rumi, that I was not a drop in the ocean but the entire ocean in a drop. I let the words enter the black box and process without bias because the algorithm was spiritual. Experiencing the powers of my new thought mindset, all of the filters were dissolved and all of the data were wrangled until the output was the whole truth and nothing but the truth.

I began to strongly sense and experience my higher self, cooing at times like a newborn and at other times feeling awkwardly curious, innocent, bashful, and confused like a pre-teen experiencing puberty. The embedded me within, and the celestial me beyond, started to pulsate in unison and my physical being rebooted with breath's inhale, exhale.

I fasted, prayed and meditated for three days. After the fast, I had an unquenchable thirst for spiritual knowledge and wisdom, not religion. I needed the origins and essence of spirituality before it was hijacked and rebranded by the patriarchy as religion. The urge was not for new knowledge, however, as I kept getting the sense that I was going back to retrieve notes my own ancient soul had written. I had the knowledge within me. I just needed to remember.

For a moment, I struggled to find accurate and reliable information. Knowing that deceivers hid sacred knowledge and truth by overwriting them in their own image as the written histories of oppressors, my Gullah ancestors blessed my dreams over several nights with clear instructions on where to start. Vivid dream memories from my youth celebrating my Gullah heritage with my extended families at festivals and family reunions on St. Helena Island and Beaufort,

South Carolina brought back the oral histories spoken by honored Gullah storytellers and griots. They were my nightly cinema. I arose one morning exclaiming in the Gullah language, "Gawd dun ansuh wi!"

I began reading books that had sat on my bookshelves for decades that I had not gotten a chance to read. Masterpieces by Queen Quet, Marquetta L. Goodwine, Cheikh Anta Diop, Asa Hilliard, John Henrik Clarke, Frances Cress Welsing, Llaila O. Africa, Chancellor Williams, Edward Bruce Bynum, and George G. M. James just to name a few. Instead of listing their works, I prefer readers look up the authors' names to force input into search engine algorithms so that they learn to be less biased in their ranking and indexing of the works of these great authors. The messages underlying the words in the texts emerged through deep concentrations and, behold, there were my missing notebooks; they contained the knowledge I needed to remember.

As I remembered, I also began to miss the support and sense of belonging of my past kinship, friendships and loves over the entirety of my soul's path. I lamented over missed opportunities for conversations the current moment conjured up about what I was remembering, and yearning for those I was deeply missing. Melodiously, I heard them singing sweetly to my spirit as they stomped in ring shout jubilee. I gleefully welcomed my spiritual and ancestral guides, and doing so deconditioned my childhood learning to ignore and deny their existence. They said I only needed to ask and they would always show me the path that led to whatever I sought. I asked, *what is my purpose, what am I to fulfill in this realm?*

They chuckled as if they thought I'd never ask, and then said: "Hold on, your journey will be abundantly blessed with many beloved communities, some wherein you will be the help and others wherein you will be the healed." I respectfully offered my deepest gratitude, honor and joy that they were guiding and protecting me at the behest of the Divine.

The Ascension Community became one such group to which my spiritual guides would lead me. The shares were genuine and meant to promote healing rather than hurt. With great sincerity, each share was respected as what the sharer heard or understood without judgment while bold discussion was welcomed. No one was hailed to be an authority on any matter, but all listened and learned with agency to freely engage at their highest frequency.

> "Knowing that deceivers hid sacred knowledge and truth by overwriting them in their own image as the written histories of oppressors, my Gullah ancestors blessed my dreams over several nights with clear instructions on where to start."

Presently, I am not whole but I am mending. I still miss my father dearly, but I now understand him as one transformed into another form of energy. This brief moment of separation is temporary, not final. My marriage is a work in progress, with transparency and honesty at the forefront as well as forgiveness and reconciliation. I might add, love never left but it used to be recklessly mismanaged and taken for granted. Now it is given the care, respect and attention it needs to work in healthy ways within my wife and myself.

The journey is not a race, but a transformative process that unfolds. The ascension journey is the blossoming of the flower of life, beautiful at every fold and bloom, and changing according to season. My life has transformed in ways that permit more confidence and conviction in perceiving and receiving information intuitively. I process the happenings around me with an open mind.

I focus on detecting heart frequencies from their source to study and understand unrevealed intent, and inviting the originator to be transparent in presenting their commodity as we barter metaphysically. Furthermore, I thoughtfully choose whether or not to engage in the transaction. My mark is set on mingling with ascending, intuitive minded barterers where our gifts transmit experiences that uplift all of us.

I now perceive negativity as an invitation to engage but with caution and respect. True to its nature, such energy seeks attention to drain me and provoke adverse reactions. It is transparent about its intentions, but in the past, I often erred by trying to spar with it, emitting my own negative energy. My record was 0 wins--infinite losses. Compounding negative energy allowed discontent to settle in. Even if my victory was physically the projected illusion, the sensation was short lived and depression or shame soon followed and lingered. As I have grown spiritually, I've learned that my mind, thoughts and actions produce the true intentions of my heart; they cannot be disguised.

On my ascension journey, I strive to direct my heart energy towards my purpose in higher realms, along the soft-tough love spectrum attuned to the situation at hand. I feel it is my responsibility to give negative energy the attention it begs, but to cast its product of work in love and light for good. Instead of honking at someone who has cut me off in traffic, I calmly pray for their safety and all others along their route and that they reach their destination safely. Instead of wishing all White supremacists, racists, sexists, pedophiles, etc. be cursed to experience the trauma of their victims for all eternity, I now pray that love and Divine light transform their hearts, and that justice for the victims prevail.

When I struggle with their purpose, and knowing that not everything is good, I concentrate to find spiritual serendipity in all things. The game plan now is in knowing I give the energy permission to charge a good intent or one on the contrary. I reside to get into "good trouble", as defined by the late congressmen and civil rights leader, John Lewis. When my light shines, our light shines.

For myself, thoughts must be tamed so that they are rooted in love and righteousness. By meditating and silencing my mind, thought is trained to understand conditions that will permit its formation and transmission into action, versus conditions for its termination. I willfully admit that I do not have all of the answers, nor am I an expert on coping with the ebbs and flows of life. I recommend great healthcare professionals and metaphysicians for that. However, in sharing my ascension journey experience, I hope that my healing aids in healing others. Blessings to you.

CHECK IT OUT

Dark Light Consciousness: Melanin, Serpent Power, and the Luminous Matrix of Reality **by Bruce Edward Bynum**
The Hidden Messages in Water **by Masaru Emoto**
Autobiography of a Yogi **by Paramahansa Yogananda**

TOOLS TO MINE YOUR DIAMOND

◇ My "go to" intervention for grounding when I experience difficulties or setbacks on my ascension journey is qigong and Tai Chi. Filling the space with meditation music invites even more relief. Through moving meditation and focused breath, I relax and recenter.

◇ Another practice that helps me get back on track is to connect with nature and express my gratitude to Mother Earth for her gifts and blessings. I look forward to my time in silence when I commune with Divine Spirit. Outside in fresh air, feet on the grass, kisses from the breeze, showered in solar or lunar rays I am cradled in cosmic love, harmony, and peace. I might meditate in nature, take a nature walk, or simply go outdoors and breathe. When I am guided to be still, Spirit might later stir to be expressed through journaling or nature photos. Always pause to give gratitude and praise for spiritual favors such as love, peace, grace, and mercy.

# DISCUSSION QUESTIONS

What do you think is the difference between spirituality and religion, and how might an understanding of each help you fulfill your purpose in this life?

Reflect on ways your thoughts have manifested into actions. Describe the passage of a good thought you had from its formation, to action, to how it made you and others feel. Now do the same for a bad thought. Formulate one affirmation you will use to cultivate the formation of a good thought and terminate the formation of a bad one.

REFLECT & RELEASE

REFLECT & RELEASE

THIS IS WHAT I HEARD

TAPESTRY

EQUINE "EQ" SHEFFIELD

Equine Sheffield is a spiritually compassionate man and being on a journey of enlightenment. He is an intellectual who always seeks to uncover life's most precious and hidden secrets; he possesses an insatiable thirst for knowledge.

For over thirty years, he has acquired and collected rare books, even those that are currently out-of-print, and he has vast knowledge in the major religions such as Islam, Christianity, Buddhism and Hinduism, just to name a few. He was inspired by his grandmother's work ethic, strength, and her desire to be the best version of herself. In his spare time, he enjoys family time and exploring nature. This publication is the first place that he has ever expressed his views on consciousness and is honored to do so.

Equine is a father of four and he is optimistic that his legacy has been significantly impacted as a result of his Ascension journey. He currently resides in Richmond, Virginia and is a dedicated and proven professional commercial truck driver.

INSPIRATION

I release all that no longer serves me and embark on a journey to know and love myself deeper. All that I need is within me, and I consistently create from that place of being.
－－ Equine "EQ" Sheffield

While on this journey of ascension, I've had to grapple with many doubts. I quickly learned that I would encounter difficulties while becoming more enlightened and ascending to a higher level of consciousness.

So, why do I believe?

There are many reasons why I believe the way I do. However, I cannot say what I know is the actual truth. I've learned that beliefs and facts are fundamentally opinions. Just because something was written by someone doesn't make it true. I say this because some words appear to hold more value than others. This thought led me to the opinion that it is no longer about truth, but more about how many people we can convince.

My personal journey began with the birth of my eldest child. When he was born, I didn't have much to offer him; but I was able to pass on knowledge and wisdom, from which he could benefit throughout his life. As I began to grow and mature, I was introduced to Black consciousness. Black consciousness contains a wide range of ideas and can mean to have pride in race, knowing your history, reacting against oppression and understanding people's position in this world, as well as knowing that self-worth and value is not measured by man and no price tag is big enough to "buy" you. I often look back to 1997/1998 when I read *Civilization or Barbarism* by Cheikh Anta Diop and was astonished.

The new information I uncovered made learning

exciting and gave me greater understanding of my culture and history. A greater understanding of "self" emerged. Once I learned self-discovery, I realized my limitations were few.

I'm now convinced that consciousness is everything you experience in your lifetime. I've corrected my thinking, perspective, perception and world views because of the type of discussions that we have had in the Ascension Community. I challenged myself more than I had previously, and I offer more guidance to others as a means to help them find their way.

> "A greater understanding of self emerged.
> Once I learned self-discovery, I realized my
> limitations were few."

Experiences are endless and have no limitations--from the scent in the air right before the rain that alerts us of the impending weather; the cheerful laughter of children playing outside on a beautiful, summer day; the mouthwatering taste of a fresh, hot home-baked sweet potato pie that just came out of the oven to the indescribable pain experienced as a result of the loss of a loved one. The Ascension Community revealed to me that consciousness isn't solely based on knowing your history, but that it is just as important to know your Creator. There is so much to be learned if time is taken to sit and fully open our hearts and listen to the Universe. Some communication is more obvious than others, so it is important to be open-minded and flexible.

I have opened up my mind and altered my thought process, which helped change my perspective on life. As a result of my growth and open-mindedness to learn, some of my best conversations about religion and science have been with Atheists. I say this because Atheists know why they don't believe. They took the time to research their doubts. Once I heard the claim that Jesus didn't exist, it sparked conversations within myself and created the desire to continue to study and research more about religions and spirituality. When it comes to knowledge on this subject, I realize I don't have all the answers. I am not under the illusion of omniscience. However, when it comes to being conscious of one's self, we must first let go and deal with the issues of self. It's not about knowing others, it's about knowing yourself. We have all the resources we need internally. Bring them to the forefront, stop putting chains on the mind, continue to push forward and never stop creating. Life is yours to be whatever you desire to create. Remember to be kind, gentle and thoughtful of others and watch how brokenness becomes fulfillment.

> "When it comes to knowledge on this subject, I realize I don't have all the answers. I am not under the illusion of omniscience."

I had downloaded the Clubhouse application, but didn't understand how it worked. I tried to navigate what I now know as *rooms* and *hallways*. In each of these rooms were different topics being discussed-- current events, music, relationships, religion and the possibility to meet new people globally, for example. Having said that, on 10/24/2021, I heard it call out to me. I was up late. For the life of me, I couldn't sleep. I was looking for a quiet place to rest my mind and that's when the Ascension Community found me and drew me in; it was an undeniable gravitational pull.

You know something is for you when it finds you; I didn't have to seek it out. Some would ask why I felt that this was the perfect place. How could I have possibly known that I was exactly where I was supposed to be? For me, it was obvious, and the date was the first indication. $1+0+2+4+2+0+2+1=(1)(2)$; and when you total 1+2 the answer is 3, which is the number completion. I was now amongst "my people". My curiosity for life and the opportunity to have a safe space came full circle. I went from not even knowing that something was missing to having filled an unknown void.

According to Webster's Dictionary, Consciousness means the normal state of being awake and being able to understand what is going on around you. Knowing your self-worth and that its value is immeasurable, this is the consciousness I experienced before my introduction to The Ascension Community and it has only heightened since.

> "I was looking for a quiet place to rest my mind and that's when the Ascension Community found me and drew me in..."

In the Ascension Community, I found a place where there was no negative thought or judgment. I feel like my views are not popular, but are more conscious and controversial, which is often rejected. The curiosity of others and individual opinions about life experiences peaked my interest. They've challenged me and given me confidence to express my opinions openly. I've learned to live my life knowing that I can change my outcome by creating what I want in my mind and manifesting it into reality. I found that I have a direct connection with Source (God), and that there is nothing I cannot accomplish. All I need is within my reach. I can change the outcome of any situation. I now look back over my life and recognize how every experience is intertwined, whether positive or negative, and is helping to form a pattern. Someday it will develop into a beautiful tapestry.

The Ascension Community has been refreshing and has pushed me to do things outside my comfort zone, such as teaching to share, facing my fears, learning to overcome stage fright, and understanding that all things are interconnected.

CHECK IT OUT

How to Change Your Mind **by Michael Pollan**
An End to Upside Down Thinking **by Mark Gober**
African Religions and Philosophy **by Dr. John Mbiti**

TOOLS TO MINE YOUR DIAMOND

◇ One tool I found helpful along my ascension journey is to acknowledge the situation of concern. I had to come to terms that there was an internal struggle that may or may not have external contributors, and

I needed to filter through some things to identify and label those feelings as discomfort or fear and develop my own coping strategies to heal and deal with it. The transition wasn't easy. I understood that the uncertainty only prompted more questions and I couldn't figure it out on my own. I engaged in exercise, meditation, read literature and communicated with like-minded individuals that I knew I could trust, and with whom I could be transparent and vulnerable without judgment. That's what I needed most.

◆ Secondly, I participate in self-care. It is in those times when we feel like we are seeking ourselves that we need to be most connected and kind to ourselves. It is feeding my soul.

DISCUSSION QUESTIONS

Do spiritual people say they are spiritual because they are not religious, or is this some way to differentiate themselves from people who consider themselves religious because they feel they are superior to them?

Is there a difference between free will and free thought?

REFLECT & RELEASE

REFLECT & RELEASE

THIS IS WHAT I HEARD

THE INNER WORK

DR. NAZLI FOULADI

Dr. Nazli Fouladi is a licensed clinical psychologist with an interest in diversity issues and family therapy in cross-cultural settings. She currently has a private practice in Maryland and works with clients presenting various psychological issues. She is interested in the arts and believes that the integration of creativity in therapy is very beneficial for introspection during the therapeutic process.

She also believes that a healthy mind exists in a healthy body and, therefore, is a big advocate of a lifestyle that includes healthy eating habits and regular exercise. Her vision for the future is to create a more inclusive approach to mental health, which includes a focus on spiritual health from a young age.

Dr. Fouladi enjoys spending time with her husband and two children. She especially loves cooking and traveling with her family.

INSPIRATION

What you seek is seeking you. -- Rumi

I think ascension begins by going through an internal transformative process. During which, a person sheds the fear of viewing themselves and their life from various angles. At that point, the individual develops knowledge of self and the way they interact in the world. With this new knowledge, the individual is ready to move (or ascend) to the next phase of their existence and to make changes with the tools they have gained. For instance, this can happen from a psychological perspective as a result of therapeutic introspection or at a deeper spiritual level, depending on the individual. In any case, it happens very naturally, whether you are aware of it or not. It might happen little by little while doing regular things in daily life and simply accumulate over time. It might happen as the result of an event and provides an opportunity to look deeper within. For example, the birth of a child may open one's eyes to a perspective where the needs and happiness of their child become greater than their own. This unconditional love is, in itself, a window to another aspect of being.

For me, it was major life events in addition to little instances that gradually opened my eyes. I would go through one big realization, and it would be quite a while (while being busy with other life events) until something would click. It was as if the universe was giving me a chance to go through an emotional digestion before the next aha moment happened.

So, by the time I joined the Ascension Community, I had already done my share of soul searching, including meditating regularly, reading various religious, spiritual, or philosophical texts, and so on. However, I always felt alone in my journey, as I found it difficult to talk about my experiences with my family, friends and colleagues. I found that the general attention span to such topics of conversation did not last more than two minutes.

Right before I discovered the ascension group, I felt a gradual shift in energy. I seemed to go through my days in a fog. I existed there with my own ideas, and went in and out in order to interact with others. I wanted to talk about everything, but knew that people in my life would not be able to comprehend my state. When I joined the Ascension Community, I felt liberated. I didn't worry about what others thought because the conversations were always about what each individual heard. I was inspired by the honesty of the community members from the very beginning.

A non-judgmental, loving space where all can freely discuss vulnerabilities and strengths in regards to how we experience this spiritual journey is the greatest gift it has provided me. At the same time, reading various books as a group, and using the tools suggested in them, has helped me delve deeper into developing personal transparency and receiving a fresh perspective of life. Listening to, and learning from, others has been an invaluable experience.

Gradually, I began to experience a different kind of shift. My previous realizations merged with the new ones and completely changed to form their own meaning. My perspective changed from looking at my life as linear to a more non-linear (or more inclusive) version. (I'll explain this later.)

Up until that point, and as I mentioned earlier, I had experienced many moments of clarity throughout life, most of which were in childhood. However, my first big aha moment as an adult was when I started to study the human body as a biology major undergrad. As I learned about the cellular and subcellular world of the human body, I was truly amazed. I thought to myself, *these tiny things are always working, in motion, and creating energy; and there are millions of them within us.*

Many networks of cells and other structures are always working and doing their job to the best of their ability. They don't think about why they are here, and they just do what they know to do. One could say that they are living in the moment--like little Zen masters. They exist in perfection, singularly and in unison, and know when to wait, be silent, or act. It's quite a beautiful thing.

Now, think of all of these cells creating their own energy, and the energy they create as a network. All of this is in me, and I am a big ball of intelligent cells living in the moment, creating the energy that is me. Now, consider that everything--including the air you breathe, the water you drink, and so on--is also made of small particles that are in motion and creating energy. So, if everything is made of energy, this energy can shift in frequency, depending on the quality and force the energy is presenting. Therefore, our thoughts are created as a result of this activity. As they change, our overall energy changes and, in turn, interacts with the energy of everything around us. My concept changed from me existing IN the universe to a universe existing INSIDE of me. This observation stayed with me for years because I was not ready to understand it more deeply.

I later gained more experience through my training in therapy. I gained skills that could help me to look at my life from a bird's eye perspective. It's like reviewing a movie and thinking about the message the director wanted to convey about the main character and the role of the other characters, or events, that had an impact on that person's life. Suddenly, I saw myself in a different light. How I chose to behave in response to events or people, set the course of my life.

I saw my life as a symphony that I orchestrated all by myself. Me. This little ball of energy in this huge cosmos, was able to create this life story. I was responsible for everything. The interesting part was that it included the good and the bad. Again, I held this perspective for a long time and never felt that I had the tools to comfortably dive into the *why* and *how* of the bad parts. I just ignored it and hoped that someday I would be ready to look at it.

> "...I am a big ball of intelligent cells living in the moment, creating the energy that is me."

What eventually brought these two ideas together was a process that happened during my conversations with my ascension friends. I think of this as "seeing beyond the veil". The best way I can describe this is through the following analogy: I have always loved butterflies. Their vibrant colors and unique wing designs fascinated me since I was a child. Once I began to study psychology, the significance of the butterfly deepened. Through therapy, I witnessed the possibility of changing lives by derailing the destructive patterns of thought, feelings, and behaviors and sending them down a new, constructive path. At that point, my vision of the butterfly changed from something beautiful to a creature that literally transforms itself into something completely different. This happens with the caterpillar's persistence and the divine plan that exists within him. It doesn't think of the time it takes, the effort it must make, or the darkness in the cocoon. It shows up for the process without fear and is able to transform itself completely.

This is *exactly* what happened for me on my ascension journey. As I was living with the flow, I entered an internal state (the cocoon) where I was able to gently inspect myself with unconditional love and respect. Once I put away my fear of this process by simply deciding to give away all judgment, I became even more aware of contrasts--the contrasts experienced in society and in myself. Many of my subconscious illusions began to surface. I gently inspected my understanding of what constitutes good and bad based on what I had gathered and what I had falsely created in my own mind.

In the cocoon, I was given a vision of my life that spanned beyond the present moment. It was like looking at a clear night sky with lots of bright stars (realizations). Each star would pop up by becoming brighter than the rest, and then blend again once I understood its message. Each represents a lesson that exists for me from my past, present, and my possible selves. In the cocoon, I exist as all I am. It's all there at the same time--the embodiment of all aspects of me, and possible selves on this plane of existence. It includes all of my ancestral knowledge, patterns, and cycles that have been handed down to me through genes and behaviors. There is also what I experienced in this life and how I chose to see it up to that point.

This included the merging of my previous visions into a new way of understanding. I understand that my body is an energetic vessel that embodies my soul and all of my possible selves. I am free to use the best frequencies of the past and present to align with the most constructive frequencies for the future, or as I like to call it, "Survival of the Fittest of Frequencies" (SFF).

> "I gently inspected my understanding of what constitutes good and bad based on what I had gathered and what I had falsely created in my own mind."

It may sound difficult, but once you decide to put away all of your previous ideas of ascension, it will begin to unfold naturally. When you look at yourself with the same love and compassion you give to others, you will notice a shift and realize that you are living within your magical energetic field. The clearing of stagnate energy will begin to happen naturally and become automatic. It will allow you to see beyond the veil of the boundaries within you. Your life, or should I say, your existence, opens up and you begin to experience your true self. You become transparent to yourself, as if you are looking at the world through the beautifully clear, shining diamond that is your soul for the first time. You begin to travel through life as an energetic force in your physical body.

Although my soul is now merged with this body, it is still much greater than its vessel. I honor the vessel, yet recognize that it's here to help my soul experience a joyous life. With it, and through the divine intelligence that exists within it, I will feel the freedom that comes with following my dreams and living my heaven on earth. Therefore, I have made a pact with myself to stay true to my diamond essence and live in joy.

I have also given myself permission to have detours every now and then. It's during those times that we become aware of valuable lessons. I am thankful for all of me and all that is in my life. I know that the universe is working through me and in my favor. Ultimately, I believe that since my soul is from a limitless source, it has always wanted to be free, so I will go with the flow and let it fly. I know that the best is yet to come.

The inspiration you seek is already within you. Be silent and listen. Always remember that you are braver than you believe, stronger than you seem, smarter than you think, and twice as beautiful as you had ever imagined. Yesterday I was clever so I wanted to change the world. Today I am wise though I am changing myself.

-- Rumi

LET'S CONNECT

INSTAGRAM: *nazli_fouladi*

CHECK THESE OUT: *"I Am" guided meditation by Wayne Dyer | The Detox Life Youtube Channel | The Joseph Campbell Foundation Youtube channel*

THIS IS WHAT I HEARD

TOOLS TO MINE YOUR DIAMOND

- ◇ Let go of preconceived ideas about what ascension is, or how it happens. Each one of us is unique and has our own special presence. As we continue to understand ourselves, we are also changing, so the path changes and expands with us. Therefore, it's best to go with the flow of change rather than hang on to a fixed set of ideas. Be ready for possibilities beyond your most amazing dreams!

- ◇ Dream big, have a vision for your future, set intentions, take actions towards them and let go of the rest. Allow things to unfold naturally. This helps the energy to stay in motion and interact with the frequencies I like to align with. When I receive advice, I keep in mind that their vision might include their illusionary fears and limitations, and they may not be aware of it. Those are their limits and not mine. Immersing myself in their world/frequency will take me off course. Therefore, be vigilant in choosing your thoughts and the energies you align with.

DISCUSSION QUESTIONS

What do you desire to experience in life?

How do you visualize yourself getting there?

REFLECT & RELEASE

REFLECT & RELEASE

THIS IS WHAT I HEARD

THE JOURNEY WITHIN

ROMANA BEAUCHAMPS

Romana Beauchamps is a certified holistic health practitioner through the Queen Afua Wellness Institute.

She is also a wire sculptor, a jewelry artist, sound Doula, sacred space alchemist, worthiness advocate, crystal connoisseur, plant lover, tea drinker and mom. She is owner of Best Kept Sacred, where she not only reminds us that we are sacred space, but also creates beautiful and sacred adornments to beautify our homes and our body temple. When she remembered who she truly was, and whose she truly was, she made it her purpose to help others remember as well.

Romana currently lives and works out of her home in Huntsville, Alabama. As an introverted homebody, when she isn't working, you'll find her at her home or out in nature. She embraces a slow-living lifestyle, takes time out for herself, and nurtures and cares for her family and home.

INSPIRATION

I am blooming from the wound where I once bled.
-- Rune Lazuli

THIS IS WHAT I HEARD

My first introduction into the Ascension Community was also my first introduction to the sacred text, *The Diamond Sutra*. I wondered, *what is this book that these people were reading.* I wasn't sure whether to stay or to go but I decided that I would listen for a while. Although it was interesting, I didn't return until the following week. I kept seeing the room in the hallway of Clubhouse but was hesitant to go in.

One day, I decided to listen to that intuitive nudge and enter the space again. It was fascinating, but I stayed in the audience. Every day, I went in and just listened. Everyone's share was like a piece to the puzzle that I needed in my life. Everyone's heartfelt shares brought a new inner-standing that was missing for so long in my life. Their words opened me up to knowledge that was hidden within me. I was on an inner journey--a journey within. More and more, I felt like I was at home and these people were my family.

The truth is, I felt lost and overwhelmed when I walked into the Diamond Sutra room that day. It seemed like everything around me was falling apart. I was experiencing health challenges, my father had recently passed away from lung cancer, my relationships were falling apart, I received a message that one of the people that abused me as a child passed away, and I was angry. They were able to live their life without ever paying for what they did to me.

I was done. I was battling my own inner demons while running a business and raising four children--two of which are Neuro distinct. And out of the two, one is on the low spectrum of autism, nonverbal and completely dependent on me. I was overwhelmed to say the least. When I looked in the mirror, I no longer recognized the person staring back at me. Somehow, I had lost myself.

I spent my days giving to my children, my relationships, my work and clients, and gave very little to myself. My body offered signs that I needed to slow down but I ignored her. My doctor sat me down and gave me a list of things that were out of alignment in my body. Did I take him seriously? No! Was I concerned that I was back here again? No!

You see, years prior, I woke up in a hospital bed from a near death experience. I was given that same list of health "issues", but I was determined to keep going. I was determined to prove "them" wrong; but the truth is that deep inside I believed "them". Deep inside I was struggling to see my worth. Even after many years, I still struggled. After numerous classes, releasing rituals, prayers, meditations, spiritual baths etc., the little girl inside of me was still broken. She was still hurt from years of molestation. She was still afraid of being abandoned. She still felt like she didn't matter and that her words and her truth didn't matter. No one protected her. No one listened. She grew up in the world feeling unworthy and afraid.

> "Everyone's heartfelt shares brought a new inner-standing that was missing for so long in my life."

I lost my mother when I was nine, and my father never came for me. I was bounced around from family to family and then eventually went into the foster care system. Through it all, I still believe in goodness. I still yearn for love. Honestly, I didn't know what love should look like. I pushed away and hurt those who loved me. Those who didn't, but matched my dysfunction, I loved deeply. I held on to them for dear life. I did the same thing in my marriage. I held on even when staying was painful. In the end, all I accomplished was hurting myself and hurting my children. When he walked away, I was forced to face myself. I was forced to face my fear of losing it all and my load of abandonment issues. It was painful.

Everything started to crumble around me. I was broke and broken. Some of my so-called friends walked away and I felt so alone. For a while, I was stuck in a victim mindset. I was stuck in shame and blame. I didn't know who I was without a partner telling me who I was. For years, I shaped my life around what others said I was, or should be or do; but I found myself alone with no one to guide me. I was afraid.

In my desperation to fill that void, I let anyone in. Boy, did I pay a hefty price. Somewhere along the way the dust began to clear. I had to put my pride aside and ask for help. I learned to speak up for myself. I began to learn about myself. I was forced to take my gift seriously. I grew my business to a point where it completely supports me. That pain--those tower moments--forced me to grow, and I am so grateful.

As time went on, I realized that despite the many layers I've shed since that day, there was still more work to be done; and the events in my life were mirroring that fact. It was at that moment that I entered into the Diamond Sutra room in the Ascension Community on Clubhouse.

THIS IS WHAT I HEARD

...and this is what I heard.

In the first and second chapter of *The Diamond Sutra*, the Buddha, along with his disciples, got up, dressed, took his alms bowl and went to the city to beg for food. When he returned, he ate, put away his bowl and cloak, washed his feet and then sat amongst his disciples.

Then arose one of his most venerable monks, Subhuti. Subhuti uncovered his right shoulder, put one of his knees down on the ground, put his palms together and respectfully bowed before addressing the Buddha. That really spoke to me. At the moment, I heard, "No matter who you are, no matter what your struggles are, and no matter what you've been through, you are worthy of love and respect. Subhuti could've looked down at the Buddha. He could've complained about having to go door-to-door to beg for food. Instead, he showed respect and gratitude. That was major for me.

For years, I walked around blind to the blessings in my life. All I saw in focus was the pain and hurt I've experienced, and doing so attracted more pain and more hurt into my life. I heard, "Be grateful. There's love all around you if you choose to find it." I was in awe. I felt a shift and it was only the first two chapters.

Another part that touched me was that after a long day of work, Buddha took time to nourish and cleanse himself before he sat down to teach his disciples. As a mom who puts everyone before herself and feels guilty if she even thought of saying *no* to someone, I heard: *You cannot give from an empty cup. You must nourish yourself first.*

Wow! These aha moments made me come back to the Diamond Sutra room every day. Day after day, and chapter after chapter, my life transformed. My relationships were changing. I became more relaxed and at ease--until *The Diamond Sutra* started to reveal parts of me that needed to heal. That did not feel good. I had to face my pain.

> "As time went on, I realized that despite the many layers I've shed since that day, there was still more work to be done..."

One day, I was in the shower and, all of the sudden, I was taken back. I suddenly remembered. As a young woman, I found myself homeless. I didn't have anywhere to go. Someone I knew and thought I could trust offered me a place to stay. I was so happy to have somewhere to stay, and things were fine until the day he tried to rape me. I fought him with all my strength, but he was stronger. I was in so much fear at that moment, and I believe he could see and feel it. He stopped. I felt violated. I felt ashamed. I felt worthless.

I saw myself and my pain in that flashback, and I broke down in the shower. I was molested several times as a child, and I clearly remember those incidents; but somehow my mind completely blocked out this one. However, out of sight is truly not out of mind. The things that we hold onto that are not for our highest good eats away at us, whether we are aware of it or not.

The funny part is that I wrote an article a couple of years ago about the subconscious mind. I'll share a small portion of it with you. In the article, I wrote:

Many of us are unaware of how the subconscious mind works or how it affects us mentally, physically and emotionally. The subconscious mind stores our beliefs about ourselves and others. It stores away our fears and beliefs about the world around us. It receives and files it all without judgment. Whether true or false. Whether we are aware they exist or not. Tucking away past traumas and holding onto false beliefs aids in our unhappiness and feeds the life of destructive patterns.

I wrote the article to help others face and heal their traumas. All along, I had a whole traumatic experience that was there subconsciously, but consciously I had completely forgotten. You see, *The Diamond Sutra* is known as the diamond that cuts through illusions. It cuts away all arbitrary conceptions. If you allow it, it will help you see your true self.

Chapter 6 of *The Diamond Sutra* speaks of the raft. To me, *The Diamond Sutra* is that raft. It has taken me on an inner journey. The journey within has been beautiful. At times, it has also been scary, euphoric, and oh so worth it. Nowadays, whenever the journey starts to feel a bit scary, I hear, "It's all an illusion. You are safe. I got you."

After years of walking through life ungrounded, afraid and feeling unprotected, this feels good. I am so glad that I listened to my intuition and entered the Diamond Sutra room that day. The experience changed my life. It has helped me face life's challenges with more ease.

One of the things it speaks of in *The Diamond Sutra* is

the four lines. It explains that even if a person only understands four lines of *The Diamond Sutra,* but nevertheless took it upon themselves to share and teach it, they will receive great merits. I heard, "Stop holding yourself back from doing the work you are here to do. You have everything you need."

We allow our circumstances and beliefs about ourselves to not only define us, but to stop us. We feel unworthy because we don't have a certain amount of money in the bank, or that we aren't good enough because we don't have a degree or certain letters behind our name. It's time to release those arbitrary conceptions and be free. Please know that that which you are trying to be, you already are. It's time to remember who you are. I need you to get up, pick up your crown, dust yourself off and get back on your throne.

LET'S CONNECT

SHOP: *www.bestkeptsacred.Etsy.com*
YOUTUBE: *Best Kept Sacred*
INSTAGRAM: *@best_kept_sacred*

TOOLS TO MINE YOUR DIAMOND

When I think of tools that assisted me on my ascension journey, I think of The Diamond Sutra.

Since I've already spoken of how it has helped me, I will share others that I still use every day.

- ◇ The art of expression. When I began to express myself, I started to heal. Expression can take many forms. It can mean telling your story. It can mean painting, drawing, dancing, playing an instrument, writing, jewelry-making, baking or just the way you carry yourself.

- ◇ The art of letting go. Sometimes we hold onto people, places, things and belief systems for years that no longer serve us. Let it go.

Here is one practice I like to do. Sit down in a quiet place with pen and paper. Write down all the things that you would like to release, or write a letter to someone who hurt you. Be completely honest. Cry if you must. Allow it to flow, and then take that paper and rip it up. What I prefer is to throw it in the fireplace. I take it to the fire! And with this exchange, I trust that I will receive beauty for ashes. Either the same day or the following day, I sit down again and write myself a love letter. I speak life over myself.

DISCUSSION QUESTIONS

Who was I before the world told me otherwise?

Whose am I? Whatever God, religion or spiritual system you believe in, make sure it's one that truly loves, accepts and supports you. Be blessed.

REFLECT & RELEASE

REFLECT & RELEASE

THIS IS WHAT I HEARD

TWO SIDES OF THE SAME

LINDSEY D. AHERN

Lindsey is. Light. Lindsey is. Be-ing. Lindsey is on a journey, backpacking and dancing with life, in flow and in deep gratitude. With breath and fire and Love and death. Curls and twirls. Reflections and perceptions. Rebirthing and unearthing the core of the self, that diamond light that shines through the shadow of separation, that slices and reminds us that all are one, and one is none, and none is all, and all is me, and me is we, and we are all, and we are none.

As a human, Lindsey is a California cannabis patient, advocate for plant medicine and has worked in the cannabis industry since 2010. A trained actor that still doesn't know how to act "right", a wannabe poet, a loyal friend and partner, Lindsey has a small yet powerful circle. Lindsey is a student of life with authenticity and truth at the forefront of her communication and existence. She strives to be her best self and tells people she Loves them often with or without making it a little weird. She deeply recognizes her two ears and one mouth, and practices listening more than speaking.

Remembering is her practice and she encourages others to do the same.

INSPIRATION

My Love for you is not negotiable, but our relationship is.
-- Joan-Marie

THIS IS WHAT I HEARD

What I heard?... Well, this is what I heard...

Which one? One? It's so hard to pay attention to which one...which *one voice* to pay attention to...the options are vast really, on what to focus on. I know it's my choice. Now. A choice I feel empowered to make. Without pills, without external influence, the choice where I put my energy *is* my choice. Bringing myself back to this moment, this body. What matters? Right Now! Right now matters. Every. Single. Time.

I had been back in Sacramento from Los Angeles for over eleven years. The plan had been one year, but plans, schmaaans...recovery was not about time. It was and is about depth and inner work. It's the desire to change and do better. It's about accountability and responsibility. I'd been digging deep for the past fifteen years. With the Love and support of friends and family and a lot of growing pains that were uncomfortable, I was finally giving myself stability. Living in my own stable environment. Taking care of myself completely. Present in my body and recognizing my reality. I traveled far and nowhere at all. Shy at the exposure, I was ready for more growth.

That's where I was when I downloaded Clubhouse. These people can't actually see me. They can only hear me and maybe, just maybe, they'll hear authenticity if I ever have enough nerve to "raise my hand". Invisible. Just like mental illness sometimes. The blurry lines just out of reach of this reality, skewed only by belief and perception, perspective, medication, chemistry... influence. Talking to myself again. Aloud? Sorry...I know what's real. I know what's real at this moment. Right. Now.

2021
(knock, knock, knock)
Out of the hallway, into a room, in I go to the Ascension Community...333...Frequency...

2010
(knock, knock, knock)
"F.B.I."– I knew my life was about to change more than it had in the past five years...

2021
(knock, knock, knock)
"...there's a movie that talks about schizophrenia and spiritual awakening and some experiences being closely related..."
"...when you were reading it reminded me of..."
"... the section in the book, *Frequency: the Power of Personal Vibration* by Penney Peirce..."

They're reading? Where the fuck am I?!
Exactly where I'm supposed to be. Drop in Lindsey, listen. You heard what you heard. Geez, my life is about to change...

2010
(knock, knock, knock)
"Lindsey, it's Richard with the Federal Bureau of Investigation. We have an appointment."

Me? I'm thinking, *shit! What am I doing? We DO have an appointment!* What I was actually doing was hiding all the pot. Hiding all the smoking accouterments. All the papers of research I'd been writing on my way to healing.

No more meds...that's exactly why he's here...should I be scared? Fuck it, he's here...let him in. Lindsey, you are an effing patient!

I opened the door, shaking, knowing deeply the appointment my soul had set to inspire my ascension.

2021
(knock, knock, knock)
"...home frequency...only person in the room...personal vibration...ascension..."

Stay here, Lindsey. Stay here for a bit. Focus. Listen.
It is November. It is 2021. It is 5:55am. You're here, in Sacramento. In the "Fay" house. Take a breath with me. In, hold, out, hold. Do it again, in, hold, out, hold. Breathe. Be. Here. Now.

When I first experienced the Ascension Community, I knew it was divine timing. Everything I heard was meant for me to hear. It was confirmation my asking had been very clearly and gracefully answered about my next level-up. I had been working very hard to heal my inner child and she knew I had her back on the deepest level. She now had faith in my adult self and my inner child felt safe. Safe to leap. It was time. It was time to advance. Time to be more vulnerable. Time to soar! Time to go higher! With or without cannabis. It had nothing to do with anything but myself. Love. Self Love. The core of me. All that I am. Divinely and authentically Love.

What I heard? What I heard resonates so deeply that time and space ceased to exist the way I "normally" perceive them. There was a parallel of healing although it was unclear in that moment. Dimensions and time were existing together despite each other? Inter-dimensional healing. For my "other" self. My unhealed self. The self that felt betrayed. The self that didn't know how to show up fully. The self with that shoulder chip. The self that took everything personally. All the ideas of who I thought I was supposed to be didn't exist. For a moment, I was free. Transcended from the emotional cords keeping me bound by ropes and knots, some that didn't even fucking belong to me! Take all your shit, cuz I don't want it! I AM FREE!

After weeks of showing up--showing up for my own ascension and myself--I had the opportunity to talk to LinLin who created the Ascension Community. The vibe I got when I came into these rooms was powerful, intentional and truthful. I felt like I was in the right place, reading about personal vibration and vibrating right toward all these little avatars and sound waves of these beings I'd never met but felt so connected to. Like all the sacred geometry I see, it resonated in my body. I felt my interconnectedness. My conversation with LinLin affirmed and confirmed the divinity of my finding this community. I will be forever grateful for divine appointments.

> "Everything I heard was meant for me to hear. It was confirmation my asking had been very clearly and gracefully answered about my next level-up."

Soon after joining the Ascension Community, more opportunities presented themselves. Opportunities to grow, to ascend, to heal. To "be" and "now" the things that I had felt in my body so deeply. The opportunities that show up to test the self that I am, have yet to disappoint me. On a daily basis, I am remembering that everything and every one is a reflection of me. It has helped me viscerally understand compassion so that I can embody it. Having self-compassion has been another opportunity that has deepened my awareness. In the past, I have comfortably been self-loathing, believing I wasn't good enough or smart enough or "normal" enough. I know all these illusory beliefs are just that, an illusion. Someone in the Ascension Community said, "Energy flows where attention goes." and ain't that the truth! It's empowering to know that we can choose what we believe, choose where we put our attention and choose how we respond in every moment. It's the remembering that I'm practicing.

Chapter six in Penney Peirce's book *Frequency: The Power of Personal Vibration* was the chapter I remember the loudest. I was pretty violently arrested by park rangers in California who were not trained in how to approach and respond properly to humans having mental health issues. Power and force were used in excess...surprised? I was, to be honest. So, Christmas day 2015, I was arrested. Living in my car, a medical cannabis patient healing from the pills I was on, feeling a little sorry for myself, frustrated. Already not my favorite consumer holiday, it's all bullshit, buying more into all the things that keep us attached to anything... anger and frustration...exactly why I vibrated to being arrested and let out on the streets at 10 PM with no car or blanket or any damn thing. Gross. A shitty attitude. Anyway, I was released from jail in the night. It has taken me some years to work through the effects the arrest had on my nervous system. I've done a lot of work meditating, yoga-ing, dancing, trying to move that energy. A lot of it had moved but some, I wasn't sure how to.

I asked the universe for healing and completion around my experience. One night, after the reading of a section in chapter six, I was pulled over by the Yolo County Sheriff. In the dark. On the river road. Alone. All I could think was *FUCK! I have cannabis. I'm alone. I have a headlight out. I have a car seat. I have a cigarette.*

I lit the cigarette and took a deep ass breath. What I heard was Tangenique's voice, "lean back". I heard Melissa and LinLin, and several other voices from the Ascension Community. An orchestra of voices, experiences, chapters, vibrations, ringing through my ears just in time. I let go and let god. I surrendered. I dropped into my "home frequency" and I told my truth.

What I heard about "home frequency"? My "home frequency" was where I could go, that place only mine, innocence divine, inside, aligned. Everyone has their own is what I heard, now I feel it. In the highest, I told my truth and showed up as my truest, most authentic self. I wasn't scared like I had been. My body wasn't having a reaction I couldn't control. I handed him the documents he asked for, he ran my information, I guess, then he told me to get my headlight fixed. He was very nice to tell me my headlight was out. I didn't feel like he had the desire to abuse me or his power. I didn't want to abuse him. It was a mutual exchange.

I've since quit smoking cigarettes. And quit feeling guilty about letting it burn in his face so he couldn't smell my herbs. I'm in gratitude for all my lessons, awareness, friendships, growth, cannabis, police, arrests, shadow. All of it.

Mental health is a pretty vulnerable topic. Maybe mental illness more so. I have friends who have lost parents, siblings, partners to suicide. I have tried taking a longer rest than I should have. I've been medicated for several "illnesses" including schizophrenia, ADHD and anxiety to name a few, not necessarily diagnosed. Are you shaking your head? I couldn't be more grateful for the doctor. Although maybe unethical, I believe he was a beautiful human doing the best he knew how and I do not blame him for any of my illnesses or suffering because I don't believe I am ill or suffering. Every day I wake up, I know life chose me.

> "In the highest, I told my truth and showed up as my truest, most authentic self. I wasn't scared like I had been."

Memories of the doctor's office. Santa Monica Boulevard. Memories of the F.B.I.. Silverlake. Memories of the park rangers. Flashes of that jail cell. All they are, are memories. No longer a glitchy vibration I couldn't seem to escape. I am experiencing through new eyes, observing from a new perspective. In gratitude for the Ascension Community and all the people who share their truth and stories so we can all heal. Each room I have shed, shared, cried, laughed, connected, got all up in my ego, all up in my emotions, cared about some people I'll never meet and met some lifelong friends.

I am a proud member of the Ascension Community and advocate of ascension. Let us lift each other up, adjust each other's crowns and hold hands in Love as we be!

LET'S CONNECT

www.ATherapeuticAlternative.com
www.CoreLight.org
PODCAST: Anchor/INRWRK

TOOLS TO MINE YOUR DIAMOND

◇ After I was arrested in 2015, my body experienced reactions out of my control, nervous system glitches at the sight of any type of law enforcement. One of the practices I remember reading AND someone sharing with me was to name my feelings, any sensations I was experiencing in the moment, naming and re-recognizing body parts I see and feel, bringing my attention to my breath, all to bring me back into my body, to this moment, to connect to my breath, to connect to Source. Although a lot of that energy has moved, I still use this often.

◈ The second tool I use (given to me by KellyAnn and CoreLight, a beloved friend) is practicing the "witness". Observing the observer. Without judgment, watching myself.

To get a different perspective, this has been really useful. In a private conversation with Tangenique, she put this very simply for me, "Lean back". Get out of my own way. In moments of chaos, "lean back" is a very simple adjustment that has enhanced my "witness". Gratitude to Tangenique. The reason this tool works well for me can also be explained by Einstein's quote, "We can't solve problems by using the same kind of thinking we used when we created them."

....

 DISCUSSION QUESTIONS

Feeling into the things we can't see can be difficult. What are some ways to recognize, listen and discern the inner vibrations?

When I feel defeated or challenged, it's easy to forget gratitude. Come up with a few simple sayings or sentences to remember gratitude to keep in your heart or pocket, and say them aloud. For example, "Thank you for the opportunity to grow today. Show me with clarity and grace what I need to see."

After expressing gratitude aloud a few times, how does it shift your mood? Did you observe a shift in your body?

REFLECT & RELEASE

REFLECT & RELEASE

REFERENCES

Equine "EQ" Sheffield

1. Oxford Advanced Learners Dictionary, noun. "consciousness" accessed Marched 03, 2022, http://www.oxford.learnersdictonaries.com/dictionary/consciousness.

Kimberly Gardner, Ph.D.

Jalāl al-Dīn Rūmī (2015). Selected Poems. Translated by John Moyne. Penguin Books. p. 350. ISBN 978-0-14-196911-4.

Lewis, John, and Andrew Young. Carry on: Reflections for a New Generation. , 2021. Print.

Lindsey D. Ahern

Mielach, D. (2012, April 19). 'we can't solve problems by using the same kind of thinking we used when we created them'. Business Insider. Retrieved March 18, 2022, from https://www.businessinsider.com/we-cant-solve-problems-by-using-the-same-kind-of-thinking-we-used-when-we-created-them-2012-4

Dr. Nazli Fouladi

THE DIVINE WISDOM OF RUMI, Brian Scott, Youtube Channel Brian Scott.

Romana Beauchamps

"Diamond Sutra - a New Translation of the Classic Buddhist Text." Diamond Sutra - A New Translation of the Classic Buddhist Text, Alex Johnson Productions, 2019, http://www.diamond-sutra.com/.

Made in the USA
Middletown, DE
25 May 2022